W9-AFG-197

Writing the Critical Essay

SCHOOL VIOLENCE

An OPPOSING VIEWPOINTS® Guide

Writing the Critical Essay

SCHOOL VIOLENCE

An OPPOSING VIEWPOINTS® Guide

Other books in the Writing the Critical Essay series are:

Alcohol
Animal Rights
Cloning
The Death Penalty
Energy Alternatives
Global Warming
The Patriot Act
Racism
Terrorism

Writing the Critical Essay

SCHOOL VIOLENCE

An OPPOSING **⧖** VIEWPOINTS® Guide

Scott Barbour, *Book Editor*

Bonnie Szumski, *Publisher, Series Editor*
Helen Cothran, *Managing Editor*

OPPOSING
VIEWPOINTS®
SERIES

GREENHAVEN PRESS
An imprint of Thomson Gale, a part of The Thomson Corporation

THOMSON
───── ✦ ─────™
GALE

Detroit • New York • San Francisco • San Diego • New Haven, Conn. • Waterville, Maine • London • Munich

For more information, contact
Greenhaven Press
27500 Drake Rd.
Farmington Hills, MI 48331-3535
Or you can visit our Internet site at http://www.gale.com

Articles in Greenhaven Press anthologies are often edited for length to meet page requirements. In addition, original titles of these works are changed to clearly present the main thesis and to explicitly indicate the author's opinion. Every effort is made to ensure that Greenhaven Press accurately reflects the original intent of the authors.

Every effort has been made to trace the owners of copyrighted material.

LIBRARY OF CONGRESS CATALOGING-IN-PUBLICATION DATA
School Violence / Scott Barbour, book editor.
p. cm. — (Writing the critical essay: an opposing viewpoints guide)
Includes bibliographical references and index.
ISBN 0-7377-3202-4 (lib. : alk. paper)
1. School violence—United States. 2. Essay—Authorship. I. Barbour, Scott, 1963–.
II. Series.
LB3013.32.S349 2006
371.7'8—dc22
2005055091

Printed in the United States of America

CONTENTS

Examining the state of writing and how it is taught in the United States was the official purpose of the National Commission on Writing in America's Schools and Colleges. The commission, made up of teachers, school administrators, business leaders, and college and university presidents, released its first report in 2003. "Despite the best efforts of many educators," commissioners argued, "writing has not received the full attention it deserves." Among the findings of the commission was that most fourth-grade students spent less than three hours a week writing, that three-quarters of high school seniors never receive a writing assignment in their history or social studies classes, and that more than 50 percent of first-year students in college have problems writing error-free papers. The commission called for a "cultural sea change" that would increase the emphasis on writing for both elementary and secondary schools. These conclusions have made some educators realize that writing must be emphasized in the curriculum. As colleges are demanding an ever-higher level of writing proficiency from incoming students, schools must respond by making students more competent writers. In response to these concerns, the SAT, an influential standardized test used for college admissions, required an essay for the first time in 2005.

Books in the Writing the Critical Essay: An Opposing Viewpoints Guide series use the patented Opposing Viewpoints format to help students learn to organize ideas and arguments and to write essays using common critical writing techniques. Each book in the series focuses on a particular type of essay writing—including expository, persuasive, descriptive, and narrative—that students learn while being taught both the five-paragraph essay as well as longer pieces of writing that have an opinionated focus. These guides include everything necessary to help students research, outline, draft, edit, and ultimately write successful essays across the curriculum, including essays for the SAT.

Using Opposing Viewpoints

This series is inspired by and builds upon Greenhaven Press's acclaimed Opposing Viewpoints series. As in the parent series, each book in the Writing the Critical Essay series focuses on a timely and controversial social issue that provides lots of opportunities for creating thought-provoking essays. The first section of each volume begins with a brief introductory essay that provides context for the opposing viewpoints that follow. These articles are chosen for their accessibility and clearly stated views. The thesis of each article is made explicit in the article's title and is accentuated by its pairing with an opposing or alternative view. These essays are both models of persuasive writing techniques and valuable research material that students can mine to write their own informed essays. Guided reading and discussion questions help lead students to key ideas and writing techniques presented in the selections.

The second section of each book begins with a preface discussing the format of the essays and examining characteristics of the featured essay type. Model five-paragraph and longer essays then demonstrate that essay type. The essays are annotated so that key writing elements and techniques are pointed out to the student. Sequential, step-by-step exercises help students construct and refine thesis statements; organize material into outlines; analyze and try out writing techniques; write transitions, introductions, and conclusions; and incorporate quotations and other researched material. Ultimately, students construct their own compositions using the designated essay type.

The third section of each volume provides additional research material and writing prompts to help the student. Additional facts about the topic of the book serve as a convenient source of supporting material for essays. Other features help students go beyond the book for their research. Like other Greenhaven Press books, each book in the Writing the Critical Essay series includes bibliographic listings of relevant periodical articles, books, Web sites, and organizations to contact.

Writing the Critical Essay: An Opposing Viewpoints Guide will help students master essay techniques that can be used in any discipline.

Background to Controversy: School Violence in the United States

School violence typically brings to mind the image of a school massacre, in which a student (or a pair of students) goes on a shooting spree at school. This perception has been reinforced in recent years by news reports of shootings in schools across America. The worst of these crimes occurred at Columbine High School in Littleton, Colorado, on April 20, 1999. In that incident shooters Eric Harris and Dylan Klebold killed twelve students and one teacher. They injured twenty-three others before killing themselves. Since then, less dramatic yet severely troubling school shootings have continued to occur.

Deadly shootings are not the only form of school violence, however. As stated by Ronnie Casella, an assistant professor of education and the author of *At Zero Tolerance: Punishment, Prevention, and School Violence*, "There exists a continuum of school violence with mild forms of teasing at one end of the spectrum and school massacres at the other."[1] Indeed, while school shootings are the most shocking and horrifying form of school violence, they are by no means the most common. As Casella further explains, "Other forms of school violence are not as lethal as gun violence but are more persistent and nearly as damaging; these include sexual harassment, jumpings, fights, bullying, threats, and forms of prejudice."[2]

The Problem of Bullying

Bullying is one of the most common forms of school violence. It is typically defined as recurring harmful acts committed by a more powerful person against a less powerful person. According to a report published by the U.S. Department of Justice, bullying "involves repeated physical, verbal or psychological attacks or intimidation directed against a victim who cannot properly defend him- or herself because of size or strength, or because the victim is outnumbered or less psychologically resilient."[3]

Education experts report that bullying is a problem in many American schools. According to a study by the National Institute of Child Health and Human Development, a department of the federal government, 30 percent of students in grades six through ten are involved in bullying: 11 percent are victims, 13 percent are bullies, and 6 percent are both bullies and victims of other bullies. In

Police pull shooting victim Pat Ireland through a window at Columbine High School in Littleton, Colorado.

Recent School Shootings

Rocori High
Cold Spring, MN
September 24, 2003

Caro Learning Center
Caro, MI
November 12, 2001

Red Lake High
Red Lake, MN
March 21, 2005

Lew Wallace High
Gary, IN
March 30, 2001

Martin Luther
King Jr. High
New York, NY
January 15, 2002

Thurston High
Springfield, OR
May 21, 1998

Red Lion
Junior High
Red Lion, PA
April 24, 2003

Santana High
Santee, CA
March 5, 2001

Columbine High
Littleton, CO
April 20, 1999

Beach High
Savannah, GA
March 10, 2000

John McDonogh High
New Orleans, LA
April 14, 2003

Campbell County High
Jacksboro,TN
November 9, 2005

Source: "A Time Line of Recent Worldwide School Shootings," www.infoplease.com, 2005.

terms of sheer numbers, 3.2 million youths are victims of bullies and 3.7 million are bullies.

Negative Consequences

Bullying can be dangerous for both the bully and the victim. Students who are bullies in school are more likely than others to carry weapons to school, to get in fights, and to commit crimes later in life. Victims of bullies are

Students mourn the deaths of classmates after the shooting at Columbine High School on April 21, 1999.

more likely than others to skip school, become depressed, and commit suicide.

Bullying can also degrade the educational environment by fostering an atmosphere in which rage and hostility reign. As stated by H. Roy Kaplan, a visiting professor at the University of South Florida and the author of *Failing Grades: How Schools Breed Frustration, Anger, and Violence, and How to Prevent It*, "The most serious obstacle to successful education is the incessant verbal abuse among students expressed as threats, intimidation, sexual harassment, ridicule, gossip, and prejudice. Racism and segregation by social class, color, ethnicity, religion, body shape, sexual orientation, and myriad other attributes that children use to marginalize one another is rampant."[4]

But perhaps the most serious consequence of bullying is school shootings. Indeed, of the various nonlethal forms of school violence, bullying has been the focus of the most attention in recent years due to its association with school shootings. Experts have noted that many school shooters of the late 1990s and early 2000s were teased, harassed, and bullied by their peers prior to committing their crime. This fact has led to speculation that the shooters were motivated, at least in part, by a desire

8

SCHOOL UNIFORMS

"Is it bullet-proof?"

Wejp. © 2005 by Cagle Cartoons, Inc. Reproduced by permission.

for revenge against their persecutors. The Columbine massacre—along with shootings in West Paducah, Kentucky; Santee, California; and other cities—lends support to this theory. In response to this finding, education experts have studied the nature and extent of bullying in schools and have attempted to devise programs to prevent such behavior.

The problem of violence in the schools takes many forms. It can range from rare but lethal school massacres to nonfatal yet damaging bullying and teasing. The following sections of this volume further explore this issue. In Section One, viewpoints focus on the causes of—and potential solutions to—the problem of school violence. Section Two contains model essays and writing exercises geared toward writing cause-and-effect essays on this topic. Section Three includes additional resources for students studying and writing on the subject of school violence.

Notes

1. Ronnie Casella, *At Zero Tolerance: Punishment, Prevention, and School Violence.* New York: Peter Lang, 2001, p. 33.

2. Casella, *At Zero Tolerance,* p. 31.

3. Rana Sampson, *Bullying in Schools.* Washington, DC: U.S. Department of Justice, 2004, p. 2.

4. H. Roy Kaplan, *Failing Grades: How Schools Breed Frustration, Anger, and Violence, and How to Prevent It.* Lanham, MD: Scarecrow Education, 2004, p. 7.

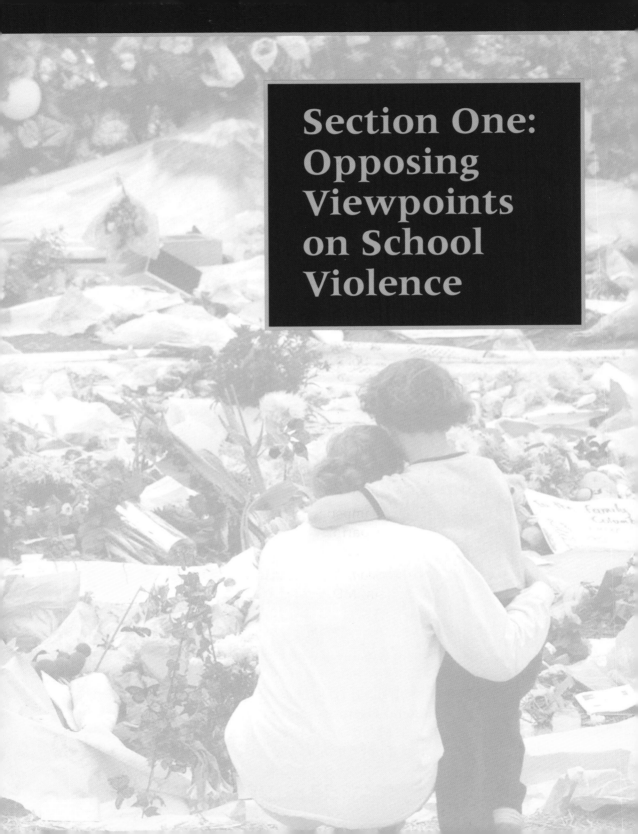

Section One:
Opposing
Viewpoints
on School
Violence

Guns Are to Blame for School Shootings

Mary McGrory

On March 5, 2001, fifteen-year-old Charles "Andy" Williams brought a gun to Santana High School in Santee, California. He opened fire, killing two students and injuring thirteen others. In the following viewpoint Mary McGrory argues that the main cause of the Santee shooting and similar school murders is the widespread availability of guns. These crimes will continue, she insists, until America imposes stricter gun control laws. Williams faced charges in adult court, where he pleaded guilty to murder and attempted murder and was sentenced to fifty years to life in prison. McGrory, a Pulitzer Prize–winning columnist for the *Washington Post*, died in April 2004 at the age of eighty-five.

Consider the following questions:

1. What set Andy Williams apart, according to McGrory?
2. According to the author, why does Congress refuse to restrict gun rights?
3. How many handguns are in circulation in America, as reported by McGrory?

The teenagers who survived the latest school shooting are blaming themselves for what happened. That is as it should be. They should bear the burden of our national disgrace—for not telling us what was coming.

The blood of the two dead and the thirteen wounded is not on our hands. We have provided security guards and the latest technology in gun detection. After the shooting stopped, we sent in legions of grief counselors and psychiatrists to comfort and reassure the trembling children. We are going to charge the 15-year-old suspect as an adult. What more can we do?

Several of suspect Andy Williams's classmates heard, or heard about, his threats to shoot up Santana High School. But they thought he was just kidding around—he said he was only joking—and they did not tell the

On March 5, 2001, Charles "Andy" Williams (left) shot and killed two students and wounded thirteen others at Santana High School in Santee, California.

authorities. Now they are paying the price. We must hope they are learning an important lesson.

If they don't, we can only look forward to the sight of more high school students sobbing and screaming as a grinning contemporary pulls the trigger on a handgun and mows down his classmates. Once again the world will contemplate the body count and wonder why we do this to ourselves.

The Gun Set Him Apart

Andy Williams was happy or unhappy, depending on which witness the reporters were able to round up. Some said he was a scrawny outcast, born to be bullied, a dabbler in drugs, a forlorn child of a broken home. Others pictured him as normal, a skateboard fanatic who could be ingratiating and make people laugh. It doesn't really matter. What set him apart was that he had a gun. That defines him better than all the interviews with his divorced parents, his teachers and his stricken friends.

The happy/unhappy boy got his .22-caliber handgun from his father's little arsenal. Andy Williams's home situation was not promising, either in California where he was a newcomer, or previously in Maryland. According to neighbors in Frederick County, [Maryland,] he was often on his own, eating and sometimes sleeping at neighbors' houses. He was not a show-off like the two arrogant killers at Columbine High School [in Littleton, Colorado]. He was an adolescent subject to many storms and moods and conflicting emotions. If he had had a dog instead of a gun, we would never have heard of him. With a gun—a circumstance sedulously overlooked by the grave authorities who vent on television—he goes into the history books. Was that what he had in mind?

> ## Gun Control: The Easiest Solution
>
> Although this psychological and sociological phenomenon [school shootings] has plenty of layers, it's hard for me to deny that gun control could be the easiest way to thwart such events.
>
> Brendan McGarry, *Saratoga Springs (NY) Saratogian*, February 16, 2004.

Bateman. © 1999 by North America Syndicate. Reproduced by permission.

The mightiest nation on earth cannot keep high school students from shooting each other. The air resounds with wails of "Why?" The answer to that is quite simple. We won't do anything about guns. Europeans observe that we have gone to war against smoking, but do nothing to stop the traffic in guns.

This time, Congress did not engage in the ritualistic hand-wringing. They know they'll never do anything. Surely everyone can understand that members cannot be expected to jeopardize their reelection by riling gun owners. And they have to contend with the Second Amendment, which provides for the freedom to bear arms. And the National Rifle Association [NRA] is so rich—and generous to those who thrill at [former NRA president] Charlton Heston's declaration that they will have to wrest his gun "from my cold, dead hands."

Teens Are on Their Own
No, there are plenty of gun control laws on the books. For school safety, we must create a generation of informers.

Students comfort each other two days after the deadly school shooting at Santana High.

If our schoolchildren expect to survive, they must run to the authorities every time they hear a peer threaten to "kill" a science teacher who's flunking him, or the coach who won't let him play, or even his mean father who won't let him have the car or his pest of a sister who won't leave him alone.

We must explain to the children that the Second Amendment to the Constitution ensures the freedom to bear arms and that some Americans act as if the red-coats are still coming, or the Indians. There are 65 million handguns in circulation in America.

Americans don't like school shootings, of course, but they don't want to dwell on them, either. The teenagers of Santana High School may have noticed that on the evening news the day the shooting occurred, the vice president's latest heart problems led the show—a much safer subject. It's so much easier to explain a "non-emergency procedure" on the man who runs the country than why more high school children are being shot.

Our teenage children are on their own. They should realize they have a president who does not wish to discuss guns. We have told them how they can survive. They must learn to distinguish psychopaths from wild talkers. They must overcome their reluctance to rat on their pals. Maybe the solicitous adults swarming all over them now can give courses on being an informer without guilt. That might be easier to do than facing up to the fact that they live in a country that cares more about its guns than its children.

Analyze the essay:

1. McGrory uses sarcasm to make her point that society has abandoned teens to fend for themselves. Identify sections where she uses this technique. Do you find her sarcasm convincing? Why or why not?

2. McGrory suggests it is unrealistic to expect teenagers to "distinguish psychopaths from wild talkers" and to "rat on their pals." Do you agree? Explain your answer.

Guns Are Not to Blame for School Shootings

Doug Hagin

On March 21, 2005, on the Red Lake Indian Reservation in Minnesota, sixteen-year-old Jeffrey Weise shot and killed his grandfather and his grandfather's girlfriend. He then went to Red Lake High School and fatally shot a security guard, a teacher, and five students before committing suicide. Seven other students were wounded in the attack. In the following viewpoint, written shortly after this shooting, Doug Hagin argues that blame for the crime should be placed solely on the perpetrator. Hagin dismisses the idea that guns are to blame and that increased gun control could prevent school shootings. Instead, he advocates arming teachers and allowing armed parents to patrol the schools. Hagin is a columnist whose articles have appeared in numerous magazines and newspapers.

Consider the following questions:

1. Why is it impossible to understand the motives of mass murderers, according to Hagin?
2. How does the author rebut the argument that video games are responsible for school shootings?
3. How do gun control laws actually help criminals, in Hagin's opinion?

The tragic school shooting in Red Lake, Minnesota, has brought back some horrific memories from earlier times. Names of small towns like Columbine, Pearl, and Jonesboro are all etched in our minds because of the evil acts committed there and the lives of innocent children [that] were lost in those school shootings.

Teen-Age Monster

Now we are faced with coping with another senseless and barbaric act, and with more innocent lives lost at the hands of an evil and twisted teen-age monster. Yes, monster is the only proper way to describe the individual who committed this heinous act.

Anyone who wants to feel empathy for this evil person or the evil acts he committed can just spare me their rhetoric. Spare me the well-intended but useless calls to understand why he shot and killed those students and teachers. Spare me the babbling about the need for us to recognize why this person killed his grandfather, stole his guns, car, and bulletproof vest and then went on a killing spree.

Cody Thunder (right) and his cousin Lance Crowe were wounded in a 2005 school shooting at Red Lake High School in Minnesota.

Sane, rational, caring human beings are frankly not able to understand such barbarism. We do not grasp such depraved behavior because people with normally functioning minds cannot possibly grasp such deeds. We can all talk ourselves until our ears fall off about the need to understand serial killers and mass murderers and it will get us nowhere. Trying to understand such barbarity makes as much sense as putting a screen door in a submarine.

Spare me as well these claims that our teachers should somehow possess some psychic abilities, which allow them to be able to see into the future and predict which troubled kids are capable of such murderous acts. Are we supposed to jerk every student who acts a little off out of class and force psychological screenings upon them? Sure, it would be nice if we could see the future and stop these acts, but in the real world, that is just a fantasy.

Misplaced Blame

Likewise, we will do ourselves no good by attempting to place the blame for this massacre anywhere except on the killer who carried it out. Yet predictably, the same people have already started giving the same lame answers when asked what happened in Red Lake, Minnesota.

The same folks who somehow think video games are to blame are all too ready to take some of the responsibility off the shoulders of the killer and place it on violent video games instead. Yes, it is true there are some very violent and graphic games out there. Should parents think twice or more before buying them or allowing their kids to? Absolutely! However, when one considers that hundreds of thousands of people play these games regularly and never so much as harm a fly, the illogic of blaming school shootings on them falls on its face.

The same can be said of the folks eager to blame television or movies for this act. Maybe it eases our pain to think maybe violent broadcasts can twist a normal human mind to the point that it snaps, causing the person to go on a shooting spree. It might ease someone's mind but

it will do nothing to stop future mass murders, will it? After all, murder predates TV or video games, doesn't it?

Raving Gun Grabbers

Spare me most of all the moronic ranting and raving of the gun grabbers who always seem a little pleased when such tragedies happen and afford them an opportunity to blame guns and gun owners. Of all those who seek to deflect blame from the killer, the gun control zealots are, by far, the most disturbing.

They spout the same tired lies about how the easy accessibility of guns is to blame, or America's love of guns and violence is at fault. No, no, and no again! The killer is at fault alone here. After all, he killed his grandfather and then took his guns. If you are willing to commit murder to get hold of a gun, what law would stop you?

Gun control opponents argue that private gun ownership decreases crime because criminals are less likely to commit crimes against armed citizens.

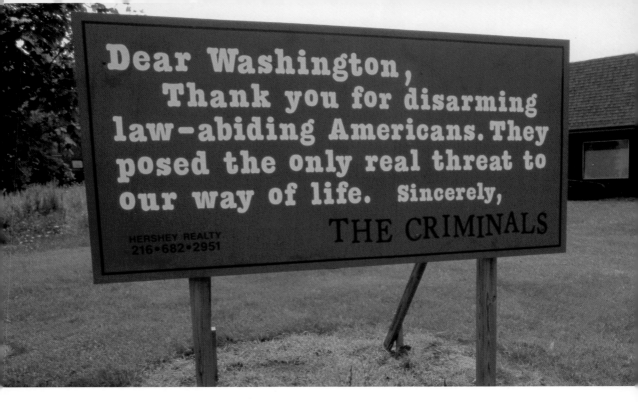

Dear Washington,
Thank you for disarming law-abiding Americans. They posed the only real threat to our way of life. Sincerely,

THE CRIMINALS

HERSHEY REALTY
216•682•2951

A sign posted in a small Ohio town in 1999 maintains that the disarming of law-abiding Americans can only benefit criminals.

The facts are crystal clear on guns and violent crime. These acts are never committed where they [perpetrators] know people are armed, do they? In those states that allow citizens to carry concealed weapons violent crime decreases, doesn't it? Several of the school shootings in recent years have been stopped by law-abiding citizens with concealed carry permits, haven't they? There would have been more dead students if it were not for those law-abiding Americans and their firearms!

Yet the gun grabbers are still trying their level best to rescind concealed carry laws. They are still fabricating stats about how many children die by gunfire. They are still doing everything they can to disarm innocent people, thereby actually giving aid to criminals. Rest assured there was one thing this killer in Red Lake knew. He knew he would not face an armed teacher or principal while he slaughtered innocents. In addition, he had useless gun control laws and Liberals to thank for the fact his victims were helpless.

More gun control laws will not only not prevent future mass murders, they will, in fact, only assure more of them will happen. Evildoers delight when no one is willing to face up to them, and gun grabbers certainly are not willing for anyone to stand up to evildoers. They seemingly prefer dead unarmed victims to citizens capable of defending themselves.

Standing Up to Evil

So how do we prevent future school shootings? Well, we could use common sense in place of knee-jerk reactions. First, allow teachers to carry guns if they have concealed carry permits. Secondly, allow any parents to carry and patrol the halls as well. No one will have anything to fear from this, except anyone who would have evil intentions, that is.

Next we stop teaching our kids that they have no right to protect themselves or others. Evil thrives where no one stands against it, and too many schools teach that self-defense is somehow wrong. This only abets those with evil intentions. Defending ourselves is our right and duty; to teach anything else is delusional and wrong.

Sure, these might seem extreme steps to take. However, consider this question. Has evil ever been stopped by cowering before it or appeasing it?

Analyze the essay:

1. Hagin and McGrory offer differing views on the role of guns in causing school shootings. Which author do you think is more persuasive on this question, and why?

2. Hagin characterizes Weise, the perpetrator of the shooting in Red Lake, Minnesota, as a "teen-age monster" and an "evil person." He describes gun control advocates as "gun grabbers" and "gun control zealots." Does his use of these labels make his arguments more or less persuasive? Explain your answer.

School Shootings Can Be Prevented

Susan DeMersseman

Most experts agree that there is no foolproof way to know whether any particular teenager is likely to commit a school shooting. However, some insist that prior to their crimes, school shooters exhibit warning signs. For example, they are usually social misfits who have become angry and depressed. The following viewpoint was written immediately after a school shooting in Red Lake, Minnesota, that left ten people dead and seven injured. In it, Susan DeMersseman insists that it is possible to spot these warning signs and intervene in the lives of troubled teens before they resort to a school shooting. She describes a hypothetical "next shooter" and explains how he might be stopped. DeMersseman is a psychologist and parent educator in Berkeley, California.

Consider the following questions:

1. Why does the boy DeMersseman describes love angry music?
2. How do music, video games, and movies affect the teen shooter the author describes?
3. How might people prevent the "next shooter" from becoming violent, according to DeMersseman?

A youngster in Minnesota shot and killed a teacher, classmates, and himself last week [March 2005]. Shocked, Americans are wondering, "How could such a thing happen?" Yet his story will soon fade from the nation-

Susan DeMersseman, "It's Not Too Late to Stop the Next Teen Shooter," *Christian Science Monitor*, March 31, 2005. Copyright © 2005 by the Christian Science Publishing Society. Reproduced by permission of the author.

al news. When the next shooting occurs it will be dredged up and included as background along with the previous three or four.

But what about the potential next shooter? What is going on with him right now? It's not unlikely that right now, in a school near you, elements of this dangerous social equation are building.

There is a child who feels left out. He is often teased by other kids who don't realize how deeply their words cut. He doesn't have the maturity to know that his tormentors are just thoughtless, miserable adolescents, too. The boy—because, it seems, it is almost always a boy—doesn't have the family support or sense of self worth to deflect the teasing. When he goes home after school, he is usually alone.

Teenage boys who are teased and shunned by their peers are more likely to commit school violence.

Benson. © 2001 by Steve Benson. Reproduced by permission of Creators Syndicate.

He has grown to love angry music. It makes him feel a little better to connect with the power in the performer's chants of rage. His unresolved grief transforms into the rage he admires. He wants to feel angry. It feels less weak than the sadness. The boy fantasizes about getting even—about showing "them."

Some days he thinks, "I'll grow up and be so successful, famous, and rich." Then they'll be sorry that they ignored him or put him down. But he lives in a world that does not value long-range solutions—even when they're the right ones. It may take too long to find a way to relieve the pain—the media he surrounds himself with seem to offer a quicker fix.

The people who are making money from the music, video games, and movies he hears, plays, and sees refuse to question the content or accept the ways they affect the boy. Instead they go about their business providing training in immediate, sensational "solutions." They provide heroes for the boy, never mind that they are antiheroes.

And, the boy has access to a gun!

Prevention Is Possible

But it might not be too late for him. Events like the Red Lake, Minn., high school shooting last week (10 left dead) and the Columbine High School massacre in Littleton, Colo., in 1999 (15 total dead) cause people to wonder what could have been done to prevent this. We need only look at the history of the last few for clues.

There could be a teacher who is willing and able to see through the facade to the pain; another student who might stand up for him; a neighbor who might notice him and find a way to help him feel worthwhile; a family member who might stop and realize that the cover of self-reliance is so thin.

Maybe there is someone who reads the paper every day and worries about what the world is coming to. This person might stop wringing his or her hands and start looking more closely at young people and find ways to help them navigate through their difficult periods, in these difficult times.

The story of the last shooter has been written. But the story of the next shooter is still not finished. It may not be too late for this child or for those he could destroy in his chaos of pain. It might not be too late for one of us to make a difference.

Analyze the essay:

1. After reading other viewpoints in this section, do you believe that DeMersseman's description of the typical school shooter is accurate? Quote at least two other viewpoints in this section to support your answer.
2. Compare this author's attitude toward school shooters with that of Hagin, the author of the previous viewpoint. Which author is more sympathetic toward the shooters? How does this sympathy come through in the writing?

School Shootings Cannot Be Prevented

Lionel Shriver

In the wake of several school shootings in the 1990s and early 2000s, experts noted that the shooters all shared certain characteristics. Some argue that these teens can be spotted and prevented from committing violent acts. In the following viewpoint, novelist Lionel Shriver rejects this idea. She insists that the characteristics of teen shooters are shared by a lot of teens. There is no way to know which of the many teens displaying such traits will act on their violent fantasies. Shriver is the author of seven novels, including *We Need to Talk About Kevin*, the story of a school shooter and his parents.

Consider the following questions:

1. What were Jeff Weise's so-called warning signs, as described by Shriver?
2. What is the one factor that links all school shooters, according to the author?
3. Who deserves the most sympathy in the wake of the Red Lake shooting, in Shriver's opinion? Who deserves the least?

A dolescents don't conceive the notion of strafing their classmates in a vacuum; they get the idea from cable TV. Bad news in itself, the 10-fatality reprise of the American school shooting [in March 2005] at the Red Lake Indian Reservation in Minnesota bolsters the archetype. It makes a trend that had seemed to subside since Columbine

Lionel Shriver, "Dying to Be Famous," *The New York Times*, March 27, 2005, p. WK11. Copyright © 2005 by The New York Times Company. Reproduced by permission of the publisher and the author.

Punk and Goth teens dress differently to set themselves apart from their peers.

in 1999 seem current again, and prospectively gives more boys big ideas.

The lessons we've been meant to learn from school shootings have been legion. We need better gun control. We need to be more understanding of misfits. We need to stop bullying. We need to curtail violent films and video games. So far, the suicide of 16-year-old Jeff Weise and his murder of nine people, including his grandfather, has fostered another familiar homily: We need to recognize the "warning signs."

Jeff Weise's "warning signs" have been widely publicized. He drew ghoulish cartoons and wrote gory short stories. He aped his predecessors in Colorado by wearing a black trench coat. On the Internet, heartbreakingly, he admired Hitler and flirted with eugenics—although the Nazis would hardly have championed the pure genetic line of Mr. Weise's Chippewa tribe. Predictably, all this dark ideation took place against the backdrop of a broken family and a forlorn personal life.

"Warning Signs" Are Common

But Monday-morning quarterbacking has a reputation as cheap for good reason. A host of teenagers have morbid inclinations that they express through art and schoolwork. The very fact that the style that Mr. Weise adopted has a name—Goth—implies that thousands of other youths don the same dour garb. Many adolescents try on outrageous, painfully incoherent ideologies to set themselves apart. In her book *Rampage*, Katherine S. Newman cites factors like access to "cultural scripts" from violent media, victimization from bullying and social marginalization. But such broad characteristics apply to half the children in the country.

I, too, researched school shootings for my seventh novel, about a fictional version of same. But the more I read, the more disparate these stories appeared. The boys had in common what they did, but not who they were or why they did it. If another school is shot up again, rest

Borgman. © 1999 by Jim Borgman. Reproduced by permission of King Features Syndicate.

assured that the culprit will have exhibited his own eccentric set of "warning signs," like Mr. Weise's constantly changing hairstyles, that if plugged into a computer would finger 10,000 other innocents as murderous time-bombs.

A Bid for Celebrity

But I did identify one universal. The genre is now sufficiently entrenched that any adolescent who guns down his classmates aims to join a specific elect. Like Red Lake's, the public shootings are often a cover for suicide, or for the private settling of scores with a parent or guardian. But a school shooting is reliably a bid for celebrity. As for murder-suicides like Jeff Weise's, even posthumous notoriety must seem enthralling to someone who feels sufficiently miserable and neglected. . . .

Surely no single factor explains the perniciousness of school shootings more than the intense news media focus they draw. Too late, we are now combing Mr. Weise's reactionary Internet postings, grisly drawings and gruesome short stories. We are rightly wrenched by his fractured family life—his mother's brain damage, his father's suicide.

> ### The Failure of the Press
> By focusing on bullying . . . , or cliques, or athlete worship, the press completely and utterly fails in its moral duty to condemn murder. And the kids have noticed. When they imagine how the world would respond if they actually lived out their most violent revenge fantasies, they know that plenty of people will pay respectful attention to their grievances rather than cursing their capitulation to evil.
>
> Mona Charen, "How to Stop School Shootings," *Conservative Chronicle*, April 4, 2001.

But I grew up in North Carolina alongside any number of anguished young men, a few of whom likewise chose to leave the building with a shot in the head. Most humble suicides, however, don't take nine unwilling people with them on the way out the door.

Who Deserves Sympathy

Sympathy, of course, is not zero-sum. We can afford to lavish it unsparingly on all parties in tragedies like this one. But one might make a case for ordinal sympathy. That list

Several hundred people gather for an American Indian prayer service after the 2005 school shooting on the Red Lake Indian Reservation in Minnesota.

should be topped by nine dead people who should have been eating breakfast this morning. Next, their grieving families. The seven wounded. Jeff Weise's extended family, living with shame and perplexity hereon. The Red Lake reservation, now receiving the kind of attention it doesn't want. The nation at large, in which extravagant media response to this killing has once more raised the likelihood that it will happen again. Jeff Weise—overweight, politically confused lonely guy, but also a killer—belongs on the list, but last.

Otherwise, reserve a special compassion for any folks in Mr. Weise's orbit, like the doctor said to have dismissed the boy's cutting himself as "a fad," implicitly being made to feel that by not reading the "warning signs" they are in some way at fault. The hurling of blame constitutes a secondary wave of violence that leaves a second set of scars. Still coping with gratuitous murder, counselors and teachers, parents or guardians, friends and neighbors of the gunman grapple with an equally gratuitous guilt.

For no one should have seen this coming. Screwed-up comes in as many flavors as ice cream, and the merest fraction of troubled guys go literally ballistic at their schools. If occasionally fatal, the combination of despair and grandiosity is as common—and American—as apple and pie.

Analyze the essay:

1. Authors Shriver and DeMersseman disagree over whether a "profile" of a school shooter is useful for preventing school violence. Which author is more convincing, and why? Do you believe it is possible to identify and stop potentially violent students? Explain your answer.

2. The first four viewpoints in this section have presented arguments about what causes school violence. List all of the causes you can find. Add any causes you can think of that are not listed.

   Next, arrange the causes into two columns marked "internal" and "external." Internal causes include a desire for attention or anger at society. External causes include social and environmental conditions like bullying or the presence of guns. Is one type of cause more important than the other, or are they both equally important? Explain your reasoning.

Strict Punishment Can Prevent School Violence

Gerald N. Tirozzi

Many schools have created "zero-tolerance" policies in response to school violence. These policies require school officials to strictly punish students who bring weapons to school, threaten other students, or behave violently. In the following viewpoint Gerald N. Tirozzi defends zero-tolerance policies. Although they have resulted in some unreasonable punishments, he argues that such policies are necessary in order to ensure the safety of students. Gerald N. Tirozzi is the executive director of the National Association of Secondary School Principals.

Consider the following questions:
1. What rules should be followed in the creation of zero-tolerance policies, according to Tirozzi?
2. According to the author, why is it difficult for supporters of zero-tolerance policies to defend their position?
3. How should school officials respond when policies result in excessive penalties, in Tirozzi's opinion?

Parents expect school leaders to provide their children not only a high-quality education, but also a safe and secure learning environment. Unfortunately, the drugs and violence that plague many communities sometimes penetrate our schools, causing outcomes that range from

Gerald N. Tirozzi, "Policies Are Appropriate," *USA Today*, January 2, 2004, p. A11. Copyright © 2004 by the National Association of Secondary School Principals, www.principals.org. Reproduced by permission of the author.

disruptive to tragic. This reality weighs heavily on school principals, who bear the daily responsibility to ensure the safety of their students and staff.

There is no magic solution to curbing violence or the sale of drugs in our society—let alone in our schools. Our elected officials regularly create laws meant to protect

Superintendent Gene Buinger answers questions about his Texas school district's zero-tolerance policy toward weapons.

citizens from these acts and punish violators. In that context, zero-tolerance policies created by local school boards and personnel to deal with weapons, violence or drugs in school are altogether appropriate in the continuing effort to protect students and staff.

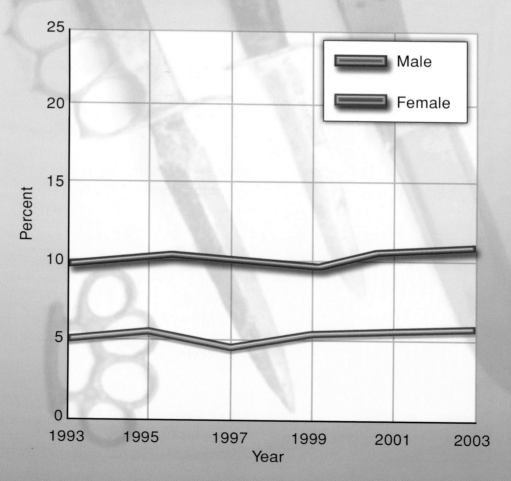

Students Threatened at School

Percentage of students in grades 9–12 who reported being threatened or injured with a weapon on school property during the previous twelve months

Source: Centers for Disease Control and Prevention, National Center for Chronic Disease Prevention and Health Promotion, Youth Risk Behavior Surveillance System (YRBSS), "Youth Risk Behavior Survey" (YRBS), selected years 1993–2003.

DRUG FREE — SIN DROGAS

GUN FREE — SIN ARMAS
SCHOOL ZONE — ZONA ESCOLAR
VIOLATORS WILL FACE SEVERE FEDERAL STATE AND LOCAL CRIMINAL PENALTIES — VIOLADORES ENFRENTARAN SEVERAS MULTAS CRIMINALES DEL ESTADO FEDERAL Y LOCAL

SCHOOL GROUNDS CLOSED FROM DUSK TO DAWN.
NO ALCOHOLIC BEVERAGES PERMITTED ON PREMISES AT ANY TIME.
ESTA PROPIELAD DE ESCUELA PERMANECE CERRADA AL ANOCHECER HASTA EL AMANECER.
NO SE PERMITEN BEBIDAD ALCOHOLICAS EN ESTA PROPIEDAD DE ESCUELA.

Rules to Follow

However, as zero-tolerance policies are developed and implemented, several rules should be heeded:

- Engage parents and the entire school community in developing the policy. Clearly articulate the policy to staff, students and parents to mitigate misinterpretation.
- Fairly and consistently administer the policy. Ensure the punishment is age- or grade-appropriate and fits the "crime."
- Assure due process for accused students. Provide suspended or expelled students with alternative educational services and counseling.
- Ensure that disciplinary action taken against students with special needs is consistent with the provisions of the Individuals with Disabilities Education Act.
- Collect and analyze discipline data. Review the policy and practice annually.

The Need for a Clearly Defined Policy

Detractors of zero-tolerance policies point out well-publicized cases of unreasonably severe penalties for what

Signs in both English and Spanish clearly identify this Arizona school as a drug- and gun-free zone.

some consider minor incidents. Supporters don't have it so easy. You won't see many news reports praising schools for an "uneventful" week. It is difficult to measure how often zero-tolerance policies prevented violence, drug traffic or a student from carrying a weapon into school. School leaders too often have been placed in a "damned if you do, damned if you don't" position over zero-tolerance policies. Media coverage of school-violence incidents raised community concerns across the country that produced calls for stricter safety guidelines. Yet the media and many in the community also often denounce school leaders for enforcing those policies.

It's true that imperfect policies sometimes result in excessive penalties, and those cases should guide policy revisions. But those cases are few and do not remove the need for a clearly defined policy designed to protect students and staff.

Principals always should err on the side of student and staff safety. School leaders should not have to apologize for upholding their communities' expectations for safe, orderly and drug-free schools.

Analyze the essay:

1. Gerald N. Tirozzi is the head of an organization that represents school principals. Does knowing his background affect your reading of his viewpoint? Why or why not?

2. Tirozzi admits that zero-tolerance policies sometimes lead to excessive punishments, but he insists that the policies are necessary to protect students. Do you think zero-tolerance policies should be kept in place even if they occasionally punish students unfairly? Explain your answer.

Strict Punishment Cannot Prevent School Violence

Wendy McElroy

In the following viewpoint Wendy McElroy criticizes zero-tolerance policies, which impose strict punishments on students for bringing weapons to school, making threats, or committing violent acts. It is thought that strictly punishing students for these behaviors will deter others from engaging in such conduct, thereby making the schools safer. McElroy contends that these policies go too far. They do not allow administrators to fit each punishment to the crime, and thus, she argues, they result in excessive punishments for minor infractions. She also cites research that shows that zero-tolerance policies do nothing to prevent school violence.

McElroy is the editor of ifeminists.com, a Web site that advocates the equal treatment of men and women under the law. She is the author of many books on feminism, liberty, and other topics.

Consider the following questions:

1. Name three examples of excessively harsh punishment cited by the author.
2. What is the Gun-Free Schools Act?
3. What alternatives to zero-tolerance policies does the author offer?

News shows recently showed video of 14 police officers charging a crowded high-school corridor with guns drawn in a drug sweep. Students at Stratford Creek High

School in Goose Creek, S.C., were forced onto their knees or against walls, while dogs sniffed their backpacks for drugs.

None were found. Although the incident was extreme, it was not an aberration but the logical consequences of "zero-tolerance" policies, defended by both the school and the police. Zero tolerance must be abandoned, especially in connection with children.

Excessive Punishment

Zero-tolerance policies have resulted in some children being placed in the criminal justice system. Two examples currently in the news: A Missouri judge ruled that a 6-year-old boy suspected of killing his grandfather could be charged as an adult; a New Jersey prosecutor's office has charged a 7-year-old boy with molesting a 5-year-old girl in an incident that the defense attorney describes as "playing doctor."

For most children, zero tolerance is experienced in schools with administrative rules that purportedly enforce safety and discipline. Arguably, the administrative rules are actually a reaction to federal threats to cut funds. For example, in 1994 Congress passed the Gun-Free Schools Act by which states had to implement zero tolerance on weapons or lose federal money. Many schools rigorously interpreted zero tolerance to include the prohibition of anything even looking like a weapon. They adopted broad definitions of dangerous behavior, which allowed for no exceptions.

Soon the media spilled over with stories of young children being suspended or treated like felons for playing with water pistols, paper guns or even for pointing their fingers at each other and saying "bang."

The Punishment Does Not Fit the Crime

The punishment for possessing an obvious toy became the same as for possessing a real weapon because zero tolerance means zero distinctions. Zero tolerance takes discretion and evaluation away from educators and mandates responses that can be wildly inappropriate. Behavior

that used to be corrected by detention or a trip to the principal's office now receives suspension, expulsion or even police involvement. What used to be the last resort has become the first and only option.

In Madison, Wis., Chris Schmidt, a sixth-grader with a spotless record, faced a year's suspension because he brought a kitchen knife to school for a science project. Asked about the case, Valencia Douglas, an assistant superintendent of schools in Madison, said, "We can't say, 'You're a good kid, so your mistake doesn't have as much force, or importance behind it.'"

And so, an 11-year-old is taken away in handcuffs for drawing a picture of a gun; an 8-year-old faces expulsion for a keychain that contained a cheap nail clipper; a fifth-grader is suspended for drawing the World Trade Center being hit by an airplane. . . . The stories go on and on.

The quantity of these incidents illustrates that the vicious consequences of zero tolerance are not isolated events. They are embedded into one of the most

Taylor Hess, a sixteen-year-old honor student, was expelled from his high school after a school security guard found a bread knife in the bed of his pickup truck.

Many schools now use metal detectors and other security devices in an attempt to keep weapons off campus.

important institutions of society: the educational system. When the school principal in Goose Creek justified police pointing guns at innocent students, he did so by saying he would use "any means" to keep his school "clean."

A backlash is developing among students who are reportedly saying the same thing nationwide. Many schools now resemble prisons with hidden security cameras, metal detectors, guards, random searches, drug-sniffing dogs, and searches without warrants.

An Ineffective Approach

Zero tolerance is commonly justified on the grounds of children's safety. But, in studying "unsafe" schools that had enforced zero-tolerance policies for four years, the National Center for Education Statistics found little change.

In commenting on the study in the journal *National Association of Elementary School Principals*, Roger W. Ashford wrote,

> The study concludes, however, that even though there is little data to prove the effectiveness of zero-tolerance policies, such initiatives serve to reassure the public that something is being done to ensure safety. Therefore, the popularity of zero-tolerance policies may have less to do with their actual effect than the image they portray of schools taking harsh measures to prevent violence. Whether the message actually changes student behavior may be less important than the reassurance it provides to administrators, teachers and parents.

Trevor. © 1999 by the *Albuquerque Journal*. Reproduced by permission.

Everyone recognizes that zero-tolerance policies were developed in response to legitimate concerns, such as those raised by the high-school shootings at Columbine. But, increasingly, people are also recognizing that zero tolerance creates as many—and perhaps more—problems than the original difficulties they were meant to solve.

Alternatives to Zero Tolerance

Alternatives are being suggested. For example, Richard L. Curwin and Allen N. Mendler have coauthored a book entitled *As Tough as Necessary: Countering Aggression, Violence, and Hostility in Schools.* They advocate a wide range of responses to school violence, which depend upon an evaluation of the circumstances surrounding each incident. The responses include "counseling, restitution, behavioral planning, behavior rehearsal, suspension with training or educational experience, and police referral."

Another alternative is homeschooling.

There is little evidence that zero tolerance produces safety. Instead, it strips away the safeguards of a peaceful society: compassion, due process, good will, presumption of innocence, tolerance, discretion, humor. . . . It victimizes the most vulnerable citizens: children.

Analyze the essay:

1. Tirozzi and McElroy disagree on the effectiveness of zero-tolerance policies. Do you think zero-tolerance policies are an effective solution to the problem of school violence? Why or why not? Support your answer with references to the viewpoints.

2. List all of the methods for preventing school violence you can find in Section One. Rank them from most effective to least effective and explain why you have ranked them this way.

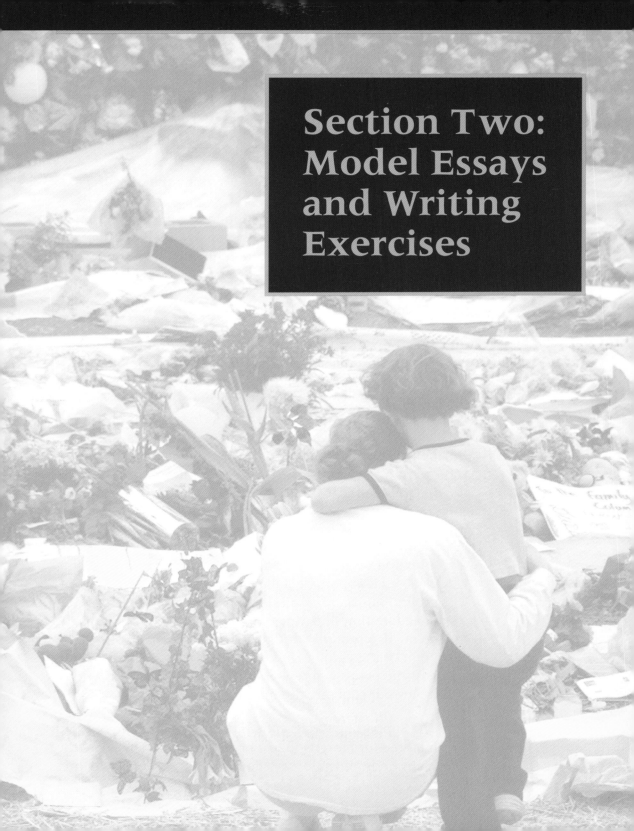

Section Two:
Model Essays
and Writing
Exercises

The Five-Paragraph Essay

An essay is a short piece of writing that discusses or analyzes one topic. The five-paragraph essay is a form commonly used in school assignments and tests. Every five-paragraph essay begins with an introduction, ends with a conclusion, and features three supporting paragraphs in the middle.

The Thesis Statement. The introduction includes the essay's thesis statement. The thesis statement presents the argument or point the author is trying to make about the topic. The essays in this book all have different thesis statements because they are making different arguments about school violence.

The thesis statement should clearly tell the reader what the essay will be about. A focused thesis statement helps determine what will be in the essay; the subsequent paragraphs are spent developing and supporting its argument.

The Introduction. In addition to presenting the thesis statement, a well-written introductory paragraph captures the attention of the reader and explains why the topic being explored is important. It may provide the reader with background information on the subject matter or feature an anecdote that illustrates a point relevant to the topic. It could also present startling information that clarifies the point of the essay or puts forth a contradictory position that the essay will refute. Further techniques for writing an introduction are found later in this section.

The Supporting Paragraphs. The introduction is followed by three (or more) supporting paragraphs. These are the main body of the essay. Each paragraph presents and develops a subtopic that supports the essay's thesis statement. Each subtopic is then supported with its own facts, details, and examples. The writer can use various kinds of supporting material and details to back up the topic of each supporting paragraph. These may include statistics, quotations from people with special knowledge or expertise, historic facts, and anecdotes. A rule of writing is that specific and concrete examples are more convincing than vague, general, or unsupported assertions.

The Conclusion. The conclusion is the paragraph that closes the essay. Its function is to summarize or reiterate the main idea of the essay. It may recall an idea from the introduction or briefly examine the larger implications of the thesis. Because the conclusion is also the last chance a writer has to make an impression on the reader, it is important that it not simply repeat what has been presented elsewhere in the essay but close it in a clear, final, and memorable way.

Although the order of the essay's component paragraphs is important, they do not have to be written in that order. Some writers like to decide on a thesis and write the introductory paragraph first. Other writers like to focus first on the body of the essay and write the introduction and conclusion later.

Pitfalls to Avoid

When writing essays about controversial issues such as school violence, it is important to remember that disputes over the material are common precisely because there are many different perspectives. Remember to state your arguments in careful and measured terms. Evaluate your topic fairly—avoid overstating negative qualities of one perspective or understating positive qualities of another. Use examples, facts, and details to support any assertions you make.

The Cause-and-Effect Essay

The previous section of this book provides samples of published writings on school violence. All are persuasive, or opinion, essays that put forth certain arguments about school violence. They are also either cause-and-effect essays or use cause-and-effect reasoning. This section will focus on writing your own cause-and-effect essays.

Cause and effect is a common method of organizing and explaining ideas and events. Simply put, cause and effect is a relationship between two things in which one thing makes something else happen. The *cause* is the reason why something happens. The *effect* is what happens as a result.

A simple example is a car not starting because it is out of gas. The lack of gas is the cause; the failure to start is the effect. Another example of cause-and-effect reasoning is found in Viewpoint One. Mary McGrory explains that a school shooting at a Santee, California, high school would not have happened if the shooter had not had access to a gun. The availability of the gun was the cause; the school shooting was an effect.

Not all cause-and-effect relationships are as clear-cut as these two examples. It can be difficult to determine the cause of an effect, especially when talking about society-wide causes and effects. For example, smoking and cancer have long been associated with each other, but not all cancer patients have smoked, and not all smokers get cancer. It took decades of debate and research before the U.S. surgeon general concluded in 1964 that smoking cigarettes caused cancer (and even then, that conclusion was disputed by tobacco companies for many years). In Viewpoint Four Lionel Shriver says that the extensive media coverage of school shootings causes additional shootings because it sends the message that committing such a crime will make the shooter famous. However, whether media coverage causes more shootings or is merely an effect of the shootings is difficult to determine. Creating and evaluating cause-and-effect arguments involve both collecting evidence and exercising critical thinking.

Types of Cause-and-Effect Essays

In general, there are three types of cause-and-effect essays. In one type, many causes can contribute to a single effect. Supporting paragraphs each examine one specific cause. For example, Susan DeMersseman in Viewpoint Three argues that there are several different causes of any particular school shooting. The causes she describes include the shooter's social isolation, lack of family support, and feelings of pain and anger. The ultimate effect of these and other factors is a violent attack on the school.

Another type of cause-and-effect essay examines multiple effects from a single cause. This is a good approach when an event or circumstance has multiple results. An example from this volume is in Viewpoint Six by Wendy McElroy. She notes that school shootings in the United States have had several effects on how schools operate. These effects include more punitive disciplinary methods, increased surveillance of students, and random searches of students.

The third type of cause-and-effect essay examines a series of causes and effects—a "chain of events" in which each link is both the effect of what happened before and the cause of what happens next. Mary McGrory in Viewpoint One provides one example. A school shooting by Andy Williams (the initial cause) leads to a search for answers that will reassure the public (an effect). The school discovers that prior to the crime, Williams had told some of his friends of his plans, but the friends did not inform authorities that Williams had threatened to shoot up the school. Blame is then placed on these students for failing to report on Williams instead of on what the author considers to be the true source of the problem: guns and a lack of adequate gun control laws. Thus the initial cause (the shooting) leads to an effect (a search for answers) that leads to a subsequent effect (blaming the shooter's friends), which in turn leads to the ultimate effect—society's continued failure to address the widespread availability of guns in America.

Tips to Remember

In writing essays about controversial issues such as school shootings, it is important to remember that disputes over cause-and-effect relationships are part of the controversy. School violence is a complex phenomenon that has multiple effects and causes, and people disagree over what causes what. One needs to be careful and measured when expressing arguments. Avoid overstating cause-and-effect relationships if they are unwarranted. Words and phrases such as "it is obvious" and "always" or "never" posit an absolute causal relationship without exception. Use phrases that qualify the argument, such as "most likely" and "it is possible."

Another pitfall to avoid when writing cause-and-effect essays is to mistake chronology for causation. Just because event X came before event Y does not necessarily mean that X caused Y. Additional evidence may be needed, such as documented studies or similar testimony from many people. Likewise, just because two events happened at the same time does not necessarily mean they are causally related. Again, additional evidence is needed to verify the cause-and-effect argument.

In this section you will read some model cause-and-effect essays on school shootings. Then you will complete exercises that will help you write your own cause-and-effect essay on this topic.

Words and Phrases Common in Cause-and-Effect Essays

Writers use these words to show the relationship between cause and effect, to provide transitions between paragraphs, and to summarize key ideas in an essay's concluding paragraph.

accordingly	it then follows that
as a result of	so
because	so that
consequently	since
due to	subsequently
for	therefore
for this reason	this is how
if . . . then	thus

Violence Hurts Our Schools

Editor's Notes The first model essay is structured as a five-paragraph multiple-effect essay. It examines the effects of school violence on schools. It concludes that violence impedes learning and leads to additional violence. The end effect is repressive security and discipline. These three effects of school violence are explored in separate supporting paragraphs. Each of these paragraphs contains supporting details and information, some of which was taken from the viewpoints in the previous section. The essay concludes with a summary paragraph that restates the essay's main idea—school violence results in a less secure environment for learning.

As you read this essay, pay attention to its components and how they are organized (the sidebar notes provide further information on the essay). Also note that all sources are cited using Modern Language Association (MLA) style. For more information on how to cite your sources, see Appendix C. In addition, consider the following questions:

1. How does the introduction engage the reader's attention?
2. What pieces of supporting evidence are used to back up the essay's arguments?
3. How are quotations used in the essay?

Refers to thesis and topic sentences

Refers to supporting details

Paragraph 1

The first sentence establishes the topic of the essay—school violence.

This is the essay's thesis statement.

The final sentence of the first paragraph previews the topics of the three supporting paragraphs.

In recent years a string of shootings at American schools has left dozens of students dead, traumatized whole communities, and inflicted immeasurable grief and suffering. In addition to these high-profile incidents, schools in America are the sites of other kinds of violence, including physical assaults, bullying, and malicious teasing. All of these forms of violence have negative effects on the school environment. Specifically, violence in schools impedes learning, breeds additional violence, and results in excessively strict security and disciplinary measures.

Paragraph 2

Violence in school degrades the educational environment and makes learning difficult. The most basic evidence of this fact is the number of students who simply skip school to avoid feeling threatened on campus. The National Association of School Psychologists (NASP) has found that a fear of being bullied keeps as many as 160,000 students away from school each day. This number appears to be growing. The Centers for Disease Control and Prevention (CDC), a government department that is responsible for studying threats to the nation's health, reports that the percentage of students who missed school because they felt unsafe increased from 4.4 percent in 1993 to 5.4 percent in 2003. Furthermore, victims of bullying may be mentally or emotionally affected by the presence of violence in their schools. According to a 2004 report published by the U.S. Department of Justice, "Some victims experience psychological and/or physical distress, are frequently absent and cannot concentrate on schoolwork."[1] Clearly, bullying and other forms of violence severely detract from a school's responsibility to educate its students. It also interferes with a fearful child's right to receive an education.

This is the topic sentence of the first supporting paragraph.

Statistics are used to support the topic setence.

A quote from an official source or expert can add credibility.

Paragraph 3

In addition to undermining the education of students, acts of violence in the schools often lead to more violence, thus creating a vicious cycle of violence that can culminate in tragic consequences. For example, some acts of school violence are committed by victims of other types of school violence, as the U.S. Secret Service and the Department of Education found when they studied thirty-seven school shootings. In their 2002 report the researchers concluded that two-thirds of the shooters had been bullied prior to the attack. Indeed, most shooters are described by peers as being loners who are teased and bullied prior to lashing out. Thus, relatively minor acts of violence, such as bullying and intimidation, can escalate into mass homicide at school.

Referring back to the previous paragraph can ease the transition to a new topic.

This is the topic sentence of the second supporting paragraph.

The statistics establish a connection between bullying and shootings.

Paragraph 4

Besides impeding learning and provoking violent outbursts, violence harms the school environment by creating a repressive atmosphere. After the 1999 Columbine massacre,

This is the topic sentence of the third supporting paragraph.

in which thirteen people were killed and many others were injured, schools nationwide began to implement new security measures. They installed surveillance cameras and metal detectors, hired more police officers and security guards, and instituted zero-tolerance policies, which require administrators to mete out harsh punishments for even minor violations of school rules. These measures have produced a restrictive environment in which students feel like criminal suspects who are under constant scrutiny. As stated by Randall R. Beger, a professor of criminal justice at the University of Wisconsin, "Schools have become almost prison-like in terms of security." In this climate, Beger and others insist, students feel disconnected from their schools, administrators, and other students. They are therefore less inclined to follow the rules or respect the rights of others. As Beger puts it, "A repressive approach to school safety may do more harm than good by creating an atmosphere of mistrust and alienation that causes students to misbehave" and commit violence. [2]

> Quotes should be worked into the text as seamlessly as possible.

Paragraph 5

The effects of school violence often go beyond the tragic loss of life, permanent disability, and grief of victims and their family members. They also include a general erosion of the quality of education in America. Violence undermines the learning process, provokes more violence, and results in repressive solutions that simply reinforce the problem. In the end it is the ordinary students who suffer the most. In the words of one woman who sought to remove her son from school because an older student was bullying him, "He can't learn anything if he's scared to death." [3]

> The topics of the three supporting paragraphs are restated in the concluding paragraph.

> A good quote can provide a lively and emphatic ending to your essay.

Notes

1. Sampson, Rana. *Bullying in School*. Washington, DC: U.S. Department of Justice, 2004: 12.

2. Beger, Randall R. "Expansion of Police Power in Public Schools and the Vanishing Rights of Students." *Social Justice*. Spring/Summer 2002.

3. Davidson, Betty Tom, quoted in John Greenya. "Bullying: Are Schools Doing Enough to Solve the Problem?" *CQ Researcher* 4 Feb. 2005: 108.

Exercise A: Create an Outline from an Existing Essay

It often helps to create an outline of the five-paragraph essay before you write it. The outline can help you organize the information, arguments, quotes, and evidence you have gathered in your research.

For this exercise, create an outline that could have been used to write the first model essay. This "reverse engineering" exercise is meant to help you become familiar with using outlines to classify and arrange information. Part of the outline has been completed to help you get started.

Outline

Write the essay's thesis:

I. Introduction:

II. Supporting argument 1: Violence in the school degrades the educational environment and makes learning difficult.
   A. Students skip school because they feel unsafe
      1. NASP statistic
      2. CDC statistic
   B. School performance of victims of bullying suffers
      1. Department of Justice quote

III. Supporting Argument 2: Violence encourages more violence in schools
   A.
   B.

IV. Supporting Argument 3:
   A.
   B.

V. Conclusion

Society Is Not to Blame for School Violence

■ Refers to thesis
and topic
sentences

■ Refers to
supporting
details

Editor's Notes The second model essay is a five-paragraph, multiple-cause essay. It argues that the causes of school shootings lie within the individuals who carry out the crimes. It is a response to the common arguments claiming that school shootings are the result of social forces, such as school bullying, the availability of guns in America, and violent music, movies, and video games. The author of this essay instead suggests that school shootings stem from the personal problems and deficiencies of the shooters.

The notes in the margin provide tips and questions to help you identify the essay's elements and to evaluate its organization and effectiveness.

Paragraph 1

The essay opens with a startling anecdote that grabs the reader's attention.

On the morning of March 21, 2005, a troubled teen named Jeff Weise made a fateful decision. Before going to school, he shot and killed his grandfather and his grandfather's companion at home. Then, he brought the gun to his high school on the Red Lake Indian reservation in Minnesota. He opened fire, killing a security guard, a teacher, and five students and injuring several others before turning the gun on himself. Weise's crime was not the only one of its kind in America. Since the mid-1990s similar shootings, while relatively rare, have taken place at schools nationwide. In the wake of such events the general public naturally asks, "Why?" Why would a young man commit such a heinous act? Often the response to this question is to blame society by criticizing guns and gun control, bullying, and pop culture media. However, these explanations are too superficial. They fail to take into account the true underlying causes of school shootings—the personal problems and shortcomings of the shooters themselves.

What is the essay's thesis statement?

Paragraph 2

Most students who bring loaded weapons to school and open fire on their classmates are mentally or emotionally disturbed. These were the findings of the National Research Council (NRC) and the Institute of Medicine (IM) after conducting an in-depth study of eight school shooters. They concluded that six of the culprits had "serious mental health problems, including schizophrenia, clinical depression, and personality disorders."[1] In addition, the U.S. Secret Service, together with the U.S. Department of Education, studied thirty-seven school shootings and concluded that "more than three-quarters of school shooters had a history of suicidal thoughts, threats, gestures, or attempts. Most of these students were known to have been severely depressed or desperate at some point before their attacks."[2] Thus it seems clear that serious mental illness is at the root of most school shootings. Jeff Weise, in fact, was described by the *Washington Post* as "deeply disturbed";[3] he had been hospitalized for depression in the past and was on the antidepressant Prozac at the time of his crime. The fact that some school shooters, including Weise, kill themselves before being apprehended further indicates they are mentally ill.

> What is the topic sentence of this paragraph?

> What authorities are quoted to support this paragraph's argument?

> The author cites anecdotal evidence to further support the argument made in this paragraph.

Paragraph 3

Another personal problem that contributes to school shootings is instability in the shooter's family. Although there are exceptions, chaotic and tense relationships often characterize the family life of teens who perpetrate school shootings. Researchers J.P. McGee and C.R. DeBernardo examined twelve school shootings and noted that shooters tended to come from dysfunctional families in which parents were divorced or separated. Katherine S. Newman, a sociology professor at Princeton University and the author of *Rampage: The Social Roots of School Shootings,* agrees. "There can be no doubt that some school shooters have difficult family lives," she writes.[4] The example of Jeff Weise lends support to this claim. In

> What is this paragraph's topic sentence?

> How authoritative are the sources of support cited in this paragraph?

1997 his father committed suicide, and in 1999 his mother was injured in a car accident and left with partial paralysis and brain damage. Several years later his maternal grandfather died. According to the *Washington Post*, Weise had a strained relationship with his paternal grandfather (whom he eventually murdered) and "drifted among various homes on the reservation where he lived."[5] Sky Grant, once a friend of Wiese, stated that Wiese "hated his mother."[6]

Paragraph 4

How does this sentence help transition from the third to the fourth paragraph?

Although mental illness and family instability are root causes, they alone are not enough to compel a teenager to carry a gun to school and carry out a school shooting. Ultimately such behavior comes down to individual choice. Studies suggest that in most cases the decision to commit such a crime is not a spur-of-the-moment impulse. Rather, the shooter thoroughly plans the attack in advance. As stated by the NRC and IM:

> Students who engaged in school-based attacks typically did not "just snap" and engage in impulsive or random acts. . . . Instead, the attacks [were] the end result of a comprehensible process of thinking and behavior—behavior that typically begins with an idea, progresses to the development of a plan, moves on to securing the means to carry out the plan, and culminates in an attack.[7]

The courts typically consider this type of carefully planned, premeditated murder to be the worst kind of crime. A person who carries out such an act has clearly had time to consider the implications of what he or she is about to do and has set aside any moral reservations. This suggests that school shooters, rather than suffering from a temporary loss of control, simply lack the moral values of compassion and empathy that would keep most people—including most distraught teenagers—from committing such a brutal act.

Note that the topic sentence is at the end of this paragprah.

To find the true causes of school shootings it is necessary to look beyond the easy explanations about guns, bullies, and violence in the media. It is necessary to dig deeper—to peer into the hearts and minds of those few teens who take the drastic step of bringing a gun to school and shooting their teachers and fellow students. These are kids who are emotionally and psychologically disturbed, who come from chaotic homes, and who lack a proper respect for the lives of others. To say that guns or video games are to blame for their actions is to gloss over the more profound—and less obvious—forces that compel school shooters to carry out their crimes.

> Note that the author restates the main thesis with different words in order to avoid being repetitive.

Notes

1. National Research Council and Institute of Medicine. *Deadly Lessons: Understanding Lethal School Violence.* Eds. Mark H. Moore et al. Washington, DC: National Academies Press, 2003: 5.

2. Fein, R. et al. *Threat Assessment in Schools: A Guide to Managing Threatening Situations and to Creating Safe School Climates.* Washington, DC: U.S. Secret Service and U.S. Department of Education, Office of Elementary and Secondary Education, 2002: 22.

3. Connolly, Ceci, and Dana Hedgpeth. "Shooter Described as Deeply Disturbed." *Washington Post* 24 Mar. 2005.

4. Newman, Katherine S. *Rampage: The Social Roots of School Shootings.* New York: Basic Books, 2004: 62.

5. Connolly and Hedgpeth. "Shooter."

6. Grant, Sky, quoted in Connolly and Hedgpeth. "Shooter."

7. Fein et al. *Threat Assessment.* 18.

Exercise A: Create an Outline from an Existing Essay

As you did for the first model essay in this section, create an outline that could have been used to write "Society Is Not to Blame for School Violence." Be sure to identify the essay's thesis statement, its supporting ideas, and key pieces of evidence that are used.

Exercise B: Create an Outline for an Opposing Cause-and-Effect Essay

The second model essay presents one point of view regarding school shootings. For this exercise, your assignment is to find supporting ideas, create an outline, and ultimately write the body of a multiple-effect essay that argues an opposing view. (A later assignment in this book will ask you to practice writing the introduction and conclusion for this essay.)

Part I: Find supporting ideas.

You may use information found in Sections One and Three of this book as well as do outside research on your topic.

A. After researching, write down three or more arguments that support the following thesis statement: **School shootings are caused by societal influences**. Each argument should pose a different societal (as opposed to personal or psychological) cause of school shootings. Each cause becomes the subject of a paragraph and should be expressed in the paragraph's topic sentence.

Example Paragraph Topic Sentence: School shootings are caused by inadequate gun control.

B. For each of the three causes, write down facts or information that supports it, again drawing from the viewpoints in Section One and other sources. These could include any of the following types of information:

- Statistical data
- Research findings and conclusions
- Quotes from articles or Web sites
- Anecdotes of past events

Examples of supporting information:

- There are 65 million handguns in circulation in the United States.

  —statistic from Viewpoint One

- "Our teenage children are on their own. . . . They live in a country that cares more about guns than its children."

  —quote from Viewpoint One by Mary McGrory

- Susan DeMersseman argues that access to a gun is one of the factors that could lead to the next school shooting.

  —argument from Viewpoint Three

Part II: Place the information from Part I in outline form.

The outline below has been partially fleshed out. You can use supporting arguments that are provided or substitute your own.

Essay thesis statement: School shootings are caused by societal influences.

   I. School bullying contributes to school shootings
      A. Provide details and elaborate
  II. School shootings are caused by inadequate gun control
      A. Statistic on the number of guns in America
      B. Argument that without access to a gun, distraught teens would be less lethal
      C. Quote by Mary McGrory

III. Violence in the media is a cause of school shootings

    A. Provide details and elaborate

Part III. Write the arguments in paragraph form.

You now have three arguments that support the paragraph's thesis statement, as well as supporting material. Use the outline to write out your three supporting arguments in paragraph form. Make sure each paragraph has a topic sentence that states the paragraph's main argument. Supporting sentences should provide the facts, quotes, and examples that support each paragraph's main point. The paragraph may also have a concluding or summary sentence.

The Anatomy of a School Shooting: The Case of Michael Carneal

Editor's Notes So far you have seen examples of a multiple-effect essay and a multiple-cause essay. The following essay is an example of the third type of cause-and-effect essay: a "chain of events" essay. Instead of arguing that factors A, B, and C caused phenomenon X, this third type of essay describes how A caused B, which then caused C, which in turn caused X. This is sometimes known as the domino effect. Chronology—the order of events—plays an important part in this type of essay.

This essay focuses on the story of a school shooter named Michael Carneal. The first paragraph describes the shooting committed by Carneal in December 1997. The following paragraphs go back in time and trace the sequence of events that led to the shooting. Finally, the author draws a conclusion based on Carneal's story.

Unlike the first two model essays, this essay is more than five paragraphs. Many ideas require more paragraphs for adequate development. Moreover, the ability to write a sustained research or position paper is a valuable skill. Learning how to develop a longer piece of writing gives you the tools you will need to advance academically.

As you read the essay, consider the questions on the side of the page.

■ Refers to thesis and topic sentences

■ Refers to supporting details

Paragraph 1

In 1997 fourteen-year-old Michael Carneal was a high school freshman at Heath High School near Paducah, Kentucky. On December 1 of that year he arrived at his school with two shotguns, two rifles, and a pistol. Prior to the start of classes he opened fire with the pistol on a prayer group assembled in the lobby of the school, killing three students and

What phrases in this paragraph suggest that this is a cause-and-effect essay?

wounding five others. He then set the gun on the ground and said, "Kill me, please," to the leader of the prayer group. He was taken into custody and was eventually sentenced to life in prison. While it is not possible to know exactly why Michael Carneal committed his crime, it is possible to identify several causal factors and how they built on one another to result in the tragic events of December 1, 1997.

What is the essay's thesis statement?

Paragraph 2

The chain of events leading to the Paducah shooting begins with mental illness. Michael Carneal had not been diagnosed with a mental illness prior to the shooting. But afterward it became apparent that he had been experiencing symptoms of schizophrenia, a severe mental disorder. Schizophrenia can produce many different symptoms, including hearing voices and paranoia. It also can disrupt a person's ability to think clearly. For a year prior to the shooting, Carneal had been experiencing all of these symptoms. Carneal's case was studied thoroughly by the National Research Council (NRC) and the Institute of Medicine (IM). In their joint report these organizations concluded that

What is the topic sentence for this paragraph?

> he thought people were looking at him through the air ducts in the bathroom, and worried that if he touched the floor in his bedroom, he could be harmed by assailants lurking under the floor. He often announced when entering his bedroom, "I know you are in here." He often thought he heard voices calling his name or calling him stupid. . . . He thought he heard people in the [school's] prayer group talking about him. . . . Carneal's fears translated into strange behavior. [1]

While these symptoms do not fully explain why Carneal shot his schoolmates, his mental illness is one of the initial causal factors that started him on the path to disaster.

How does the first sentence of the third paragraph show a causal connection between the ideas in paragraphs 2 and 3?

Paragraph 3

Carneal's rejection at school, along with mental illness, made him especially vulnerable. Carneal was considered a class clown and a prankster. Although he had friends, he was never fully a part of any social group. In addition, because he was physically small, socially awkward, and wore glasses, he was a prime target for bullying and teasing. Eighth grade, a year before the shooting, was a particularly bad time for him. Dewey Cornell, a psychiatrist who interviewed Carneal after the shooting, writes,

> In eighth grade, he started to feel isolated and unpopular with his peers. Students made fun of his clothing and glasses and called him a "nerd." In the school washroom, larger boys would pick on him by flicking water on him and threatening him. . . . Two older boys in particular who had been held back a grade . . . would spit on him and then dare him to hit them. [2]

The worst event of eighth grade was the publication of a comment in the school newspaper implying that Carneal was gay. According to Katherine S. Newman, a Princeton sociologist who conducted an in-depth study of the Paducah shooting, this incident "precipitated an avalanche of bullying, teasing, and humiliation that followed Michael for the rest of middle school." He was repeatedly called "gay" and "faggot." Newman also notes that Carneal did not fight back or seek help from authorities but instead "buried his rage." [3]

Paragraph 4

As a result of the despair and humiliation he experienced in eighth grade, Carneal's grades dropped significantly. He had tested with an IQ of 120 (above average) but was not living up to his parents' and teachers' expectations. He was greatly overshadowed by his older sister, Kelly, who was valedictorian of her high school class, a member of the marching band and choir, and a regular contributor to the school newspaper. While Carneal's grades improved slightly in the ninth grade, they still paled in comparison with his sister's achievements, a fact that

What information is used to support the argument in paragraph 3?

What authority is quoted in paragraph 3?

What is the topic sentence for this paragraph?

was pointed out to him by his teachers. As a result, Carneal's academic shortcomings added to his general sense of incompetence.

Paragraph 5

What words are used to signal a transition to the next topic?

Just as his academic achievements failed to significantly improve, his social struggles continued in high school. His efforts to gain acceptance into various social groups at Heath High School failed. These groups included the school's band members, the "preps" (popular students), and the "good" kids (Christians who met and prayed in the school lobby every morning). His inability to gain acceptance by these groups led him to seek the approval of the school's most rebellious group, the so-called Goths or freaks. As Newman states,

What is the topic sentence for this paragraph?

> In this loose collection of older boys who dressed in black, listened to dark, grunge rock music, and affected an attractive, dangerous aura, Michael found the antithesis of [his sister] Kelly's friends, those high-achieving, churchgoing, popular kids. He was desperate to claim a place among the "freaks" who had rejected the very same people who were busily rejecting Michael.[4]

Unfortunately, Carneal was not fully accepted by this group, either. As Newman puts it, he "was tolerated, but not exactly embraced."[5] In an attempt to win them over, he stole money, CDs, and a fax machine for them.

Paragraph 6

What words are used in this paragraph to signal a chain of events?

Carneal's attempts to impress the Goths led him to commit an act that brought him one step closer to the shooting—stealing guns and bringing them to school. It is unclear where the idea of committing a school shooting came from and what role the Goths had in planning it. It is known that they all fantasized together about taking over a shopping mall or the school at gunpoint. It is also known that the leader of the Goths encouraged Carneal to obtain guns for them. But it is unknown whether the other members of the group truly intended to carry out a crime, were merely fantasizing, or were simply playing a trick on Carneal. Whatever the plan, it was Carneal's desperate need for acceptance that led him to steal the guns and bring them to school.

Paragraph 7

The Goths were not impressed, however, and it was their lack of respect for Carneal's actions that ultimately led him to pull the trigger. When Carneal brought the guns to school and joined the Goths in their usual place in the hallway near the prayer circle, they did not respond as Carneal had hoped. He had imagined that, at the very least, the act of bringing the weapons (along with hundreds of rounds of ammunition) would be enough to cement him as a member of this rebellious group. Instead, the Goths talked about the guns briefly and then changed the subject. According to Newman, Carneal "interpreted this as a personal slight and a betrayal."[6] It was the last link in the causal chain leading to the shooting. As Carneal himself later explained when asked why he had committed the crime, "I guess it was because they ignored me. I had guns, I brought them to school, I showed them to them, and they were still ignoring me."[7] In response, Carneal took out the pistol and fired eight rounds.

> What is the topic sentence of this paragraph?

Paragraph 8

Thus it was a series of rejections by various social groups—first by his middle school peers, then by the high school band, the preps, the good kids, and the Goths—that compelled Michael Carneal to carry out the shooting. His insecurity and desperate need for acceptance drove him from one group to another only to meet with rejection after rejection. Throughout the process his mental illness caused him to exaggerate and make irrational decisions, including the fateful decisions to steal guns, bring them to school, and use them on his peers.

> How does this paragraph restate the essay's main thesis?

Paragraph 9

It must be noted that in one important respect, the Paducah shooting was different from other shootings in which bullied and aggrieved teens take out their vengeance on those who have tormented them. Carneal did not target people who had victimized him; he simply fired randomly into the crowd. He was motivated not by a desire for revenge, but a need for attention, acceptance, and respect. As the NRC/IM report concludes:

> As Carneal himself has said, the shooting was not retribution for past wrongs done to him. Instead it was an attention-getting act that he thought would bring him the power and respect that he deserved. . . . The shooting gave him a very public way of asserting power and winning respect from all of the groups in which he felt only marginally included.[8]

Paragraph 10

What is the main point of this paragraph? How does it relate to the rest of the essay?

The purpose of piecing together the chain of events that resulted in the Paducah shooting is not to excuse or explain away Carneal's actions. By looking at the behavior of one school shooter in depth it is possible to draw specific conclusions about the phenomena of school shootings. While this school shooting cannot be attributed to any one cause, it is clear that bullying and intimidation played a major role in the alienation and social marginalization that contributed to the crime. In addition, Carneal's mental illness appears to have made him especially vulnerable to the effects of this rejection. Thus schools should make every conceivable effort to ensure that all of their students are treated with dignity and that students who show signs of mental illness receive the treatment they need. As stated by Sam Chaltain and Molly McCloskey, codirectors of the First Amendment Schools Project, "We must . . . begin a deeper discussion about the role schools play in students' mental health."[9]

What is the main conclusion of the essay?

Notes

1. National Research Council and Institute of Medicine. *Deadly Lessons: Understanding Lethal School Violence.* Ed. Mark H. Moore et al. Washington, DC: National Academies Press, 2003: 150.

2. Quoted in Newman, Katherine S. *Rampage: The Social Roots of School Shootings.* New York: Basic Books, 2004: 27.

3. Newman. *Rampage:* 27.

4. Newman. *Rampage:* 29.

5. Newman. *Rampage:* 29.

6. Newman. *Rampage:* 32.

7. Quoted in Blank, Jonah. "The Kid No One Noticed: Guns, He Concluded, Would Get His Classmates' Attention." *U.S. News & World Report* 12 Oct. 1998.

8. National Research Council and Institute of Medicine. *Deadly Lessons.* 147, 149.

9. Chaltain, Sam, and Molly McCloskey. "Red Lake Shooting: No More Quick Fixes." *USA Today* 30 Mar. 2005: A13.

Exercise A: Examining Introductions and Conclusions

Every essay features introductory and concluding paragraphs that are used to frame the main ideas. Along with presenting the essay's thesis statement, well-written introductions should grab the attention of the reader and make it clear why the topic being explored is important. The conclusion reiterates the essay's thesis and is also the last chance for the writer to make an impression on the reader. Strong introductions and conclusions can greatly enhance an essay's effect on an audience.

The Introduction

There are several techniques that can be used to craft an introductory paragraph. An essay can start with

- an anecdote: a brief story that illustrates a point relevant to the topic;
- startling information: facts or statistics that elucidate the point of the essay;
- setting up and knocking down a position: a position or claim believed by proponents of one side of a controversy, followed by statements that challenge that claim;
- historical perspective: an example of the way things used to be that leads into a discussion of how or why things work differently now;
- summary information: general introductory information about the topic that feeds into the essay's thesis statement.

1. Reread the introductory paragraphs of the model essays and of the viewpoints in Section One. Identify which of the techniques described above are used in these essays. How do they grab the attention of the reader? Are their thesis statements clearly presented?

2. Write an introduction for the essay you have outlined and partially written in the previous exercise using one of the techniques described above.

The Conclusion

The conclusion brings the essay to a close by summarizing or returning to its main ideas. Good conclusions, however, go beyond simply repeating these ideas. Strong conclusions explore a topic's broader implications and reiterate why it is important to consider. They may frame the essay by returning to an anecdote featured in the opening paragraph. Or they may close with a quotation or refer back to an event in the essay. In opinionated essays, the conclusion can reiterate which side the essay is taking or ask the reader to reconsider a previously held position on the subject.

1. Reread the concluding paragraphs of the model essays and of the viewpoints in Section One. Which were most effective in driving their arguments home to the reader? What sorts of techniques did they use to do this? Did they appeal emotionally to the reader, or bookend an idea or event referenced elsewhere in the essay?
2. Write a conclusion for the essay you have outlined and partially written in the previous exercise using one of the techniques described above.

Author's Checklist

✔ Review the five-paragraph essay you wrote.
✔ Make sure it has a clear introduction that draws the reader in and contains a thesis statement that concisely expresses what your essay is about.
✔ Evaluate the paragraphs and make sure they each have clear topic sentences that are well supported by interesting and relevant details.
✔ Check that you have used compelling and authoritative quotes to enliven the essay.
✔ Finally, be sure you have a solid conclusion that uses one of the techniques presented in this exercise.

Exercise B: Using Quotations to Enliven Your Essay

No essay is complete without quotations. Get in the habit of using quotes to support at least some of the ideas in your essays. Quotes do not need to appear in every paragraph but should appear often enough so that the essay contains voices aside from your own. When you write, use quotations to accomplish the following:

- Provide expert knowledge that you are not necessarily in the position to have.
- Add interest with lively or passionate passages.
- Include a particularly well-written point that gets to the heart of the matter.
- Supply statistics or facts that have been derived from someone's research.
- Deliver anecdotes that illustrate the point you are trying to make.
- Express first-person testimony.

Now reread the essays presented in all sections of this book and find at least one example of each of the above quotation types.

There are a few important things to remember when using quotations:

- Note your sources' qualifications and biases. This way your reader can identify the person you have quoted and can put his or her words in a context.
- Put any quoted material within proper quotation marks. Failing to attribute quotes to their authors constitutes plagiarism, which is when an author takes someone else's words or ideas and presents them as his or her own. Plagiarism is a very serious infraction and must be avoided at all costs.
- Quotes cannot replace narrative. They should be used to emphasize or summarize a point already made by the writer.
- Do not string quotes together. All quotes need to be buffered by original writing that introduces them and puts them in context.

Write Your Own Five-Paragraph Cause-and-Effect Essay

Using the information from this book, write your own five-paragraph cause-and-effect essay that deals with the subject of school violence. The following steps are suggestions on how to get started.

Step One: Choose your topic.
The first step is to decide what topic to write your essay on. Is there any aspect of the subject that particularly fascinates you? Is there an issue you strongly support or feel strongly against? Is there a topic you would like to learn more about? Ask yourself such questions before selecting your essay topic. Refer to Appendix D: Sample Essay Topics if you need help selecting a topic.

Step Two: Write down questions and answers about the topic.
Before you begin writing, you will need to think carefully about what ideas your essay will contain. This is a process known as brainstorming. Brainstorming involves asking yourself questions and coming up with ideas to discuss in your essay. Possible questions that will help you with the brainstorming process include:

- Why is this topic important?
- Why should people be interested in this topic?
- How can I make this essay interesting to the reader?
- What question am I going to address in this paragraph or essay?
- What facts, ideas, or quotes can I use to support the answer to my question?
- Will the question's answer reveal a preference for one subject over another?

Questions especially for cause-and-effect essays include:

- What are the causes of the topic being examined?
- What are the effects of the topic being examined?

- Are there single or multiple causes?
- Are there single or multiple effects?
- Is a chain of events involved?

Step Three: Gather facts and ideas related to your topic.
This book contains several places to find information, including the viewpoints and the appendixes. In addition, you may want to research the books, articles, and Web sites listed in Section Three or do additional research in your local library.

Step Four: Develop a workable thesis statement.
Use what you have written down in steps two and three to help you articulate the main point or argument you want to make in your essay. It should be expressed in a clear sentence and make an arguable or supportable point.

Examples:
School Violence Is Caused by America's Fascination with Violence

> (This could be the thesis statement of a cause-and-effect essay that examines three ways that America's fixation with violence contributes to the problem.)

The Effects of School Shootings on Nonconformist Youths.

> (This could be the thesis statement of a cause-and-effect essay that examines three ways that school shootings have affected the lives of teens who do not fit neatly into the mainstream.)

Step Five: Write an outline or diagram.
1. Write the thesis statement at the top of the outline.
2. Write roman numerals I, II, and III on the left side of the page with A, B, and C under each numeral.
3. Next to each roman numeral, write down the best ideas you came up with in step three. These should

all directly relate to and support the thesis statement.

4. Next to each letter write down information that supports that particular idea.

Step Six: Write the three supporting paragraphs.

Use your outline to write the three supporting paragraphs. Write down the main idea of each paragraph in sentence form. Do the same thing for the supporting points of information. Each sentence should support the paragraph of the topic. Be sure you have relevant and interesting details, facts, and quotes. Use transitions when you move from idea to idea to keep the text fluid. Sometimes, although not always, paragraphs can include a concluding or summary sentence that restates the paragraph's argument.

Step Seven: Write the introduction and conclusion.

See Exercise 3A for information on writing introductions and conclusions.

Step Eight: Read and rewrite.

As you read, check your essay for the following:

✔ Does the essay maintain a consistent tone?

✔ Do all sentences serve to reinforce your general thesis or your paragraph theses?

✔ Do all paragraphs flow from one to the other? Do you need to add transition words or phrases?

✔ Have you quoted from reliable, authoritative, and interesting sources?

✔ Is there a sense of progression throughout the essay?

✔ Does the essay get bogged down in too much detail or irrelevant material?

✔ Does your introduction grab the reader's attention?

✔ Does your conclusion reflect back on any previously discussed material or give the essay a sense of closure?

✔ Are there any spelling or grammatical errors?

Tips on Writing Effective Cause-and-Effect Essays

✔ You do not need to describe every possible cause of an event or phenomenon. Focus on the most important ones that support your thesis statement.

✔ Vary your sentence structure; avoid repeating yourself.

✔ Maintain a professional, objective tone of voice. Avoid sounding uncertain or insulting.

✔ Anticipate what the reader's counterarguments may be and answer them.

✔ Use sources that state facts and evidence.

✔ Avoid assumptions or generalizations without evidence.

✔ Aim for clear, fluid, well-written sentences that together make up an essay that is informative, interesting, and memorable.

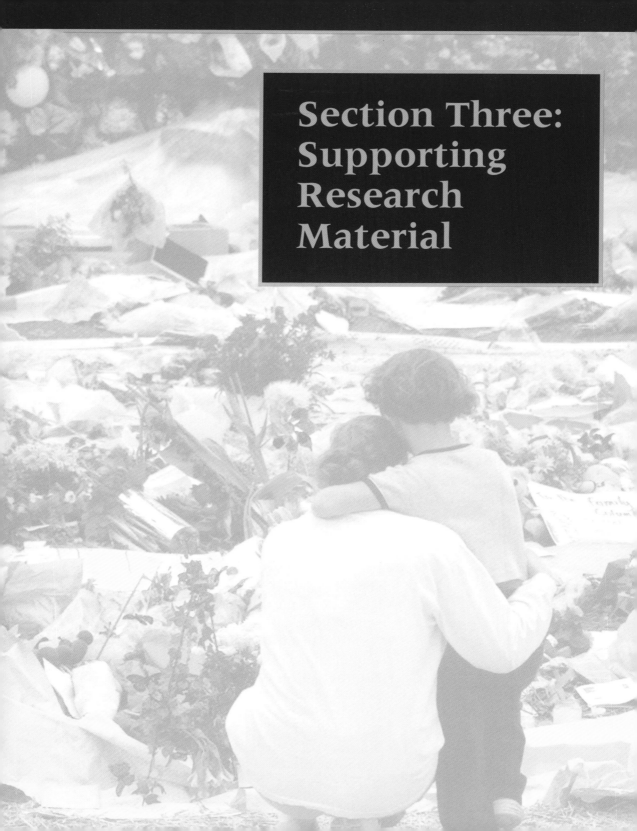

Section Three: Supporting Research Material

Facts About School Violence

Editor's Note: These facts can be used in reports or papers to reinforce or add credibility when making important points or claims.

School Violence

The following statistics have been compiled by the U.S. Departments of Education and Justice:

- Violent crimes committed against students declined 50 percent from 1992 to 2002. In 1992, 48 per 1,000 students were victims of rape, sexual assault, physical assault, or robbery. In 2002, that number was 24 per 1,000 students.
- Listed below are the numbers of students aged 5 to 19 murdered at school (includes students traveling to or from school or a school-sponsored event):
  - Number of murders during the 2002–2003 school year: 16
  - Number of murders during the 2001–2002 school year: 14
  - Number of murders during the 2000–2001 school year: 10
  - Number of murders during the 1999–2000 school year: 16
  - Number of murders during the 1998–1999 school year: 33
  - Number of murders during the 1997–1998 school year: 34
  - Number of murders during the 1996–1997 school year: 28
  - Number of murders during the 1995–1996 school year: 32
  - Number of murders during the 1994–1995 school year: 28

- Number of murders during the 1993–1994 school year: 29
- Number of murders during the 1992–1993 school year: 34

- The percentage of students in grades 9–12 who reported fighting at school declined from 16 percent to 13 percent from 1993 to 2003.
- The percentage of high school students who reported carrying weapons to school declined from 12 percent in 1993 to 6 percent in 2003.
- In every year studied between 1993 and 2003, 7–9 percent of high school students reported being threatened or injured with a weapon such as a gun, knife, or club on school property.
- In 1999–2000, 20 percent of all public schools experienced one or more serious violent crime such as rape, sexual assault, robbery, and aggravated assault. Seventy-one percent reported violent incidents.
- In 2003, 21 percent of students aged 12–18 reported that street gangs were present at their schools.
- Over the five-year period from 1998 to 2002, teachers were the victims of ninety thousand violent crimes at school. Urban teachers were more likely to be victims than rural and suburban teachers.
- The number of students who reported being afraid of being attacked at school or on the way to or from school decreased from 12 percent in 1995 to 6 percent in 2001 and remained at 6 percent in 2003.

According to the U.S. Centers for Disease Control and Prevention,

- fewer than 1 percent of all homicides among school-age children occur on or around school grounds or on the way to or from school;
- the number of students who missed school because they feel unsafe increased from 4.4 percent in 1993 to 5.4 percent in 2003.

A study by the National Research Council and the Institute of Medicine found that the perpetrators of six out of eight school shootings had serious mental health problems, including schizophrenia, clinical depression, and personality disorders. All eight school shooters had easy access to guns.

Bullying

The U.S. Department of Health and Human Services offers the following facts about bullying:

- Bullying happens when someone hurts or scares another person on purpose and the person being bullied has a hard time defending him- or herself. Usually, bullying happens over and over. It includes
  - punching, shoving, and other acts that hurt people physically;
  - spreading bad rumors about people;
  - keeping certain people out of a "group";
  - teasing people in a mean way;
  - getting certain people to "gang up" on others.
- Bullying also can happen online or electronically. "Cyberbullying" is when children or teens bully each other using the Internet, mobile phones, or other cyber technology. This can include
  - sending mean text, e-mail, or instant messages;
  - posting nasty pictures or messages about others in blogs or on Web sites;
  - using someone else's user name to spread rumors or lies about someone.
- Studies show that between 15 and 25 percent of U.S. students are bullied with some frequency ("sometimes or more often") while 15 to 20 percent report that they bully others with some frequency.
- Boys are more likely than girls to bully others.

- Girls frequently report being bullied by both boys and girls, but boys are most often bullied only by other boys.
- Children and youth who are bullied are more likely than other children to be depressed, lonely, anxious, have low self-esteem, feel unwell, and think about suicide.

According to the U.S. Departments of Education and Justice, 7 percent of students aged 12–18 reported they had been bullied at school in 2003. Rural students were more likely to be bullied than suburban or urban students.

Finding and Using Sources of Information

No matter what type of essay you are writing, it is necessary to find information to support your point of view. You can use sources such as books, magazine articles, newspaper articles, and online articles.

Using Books and Articles

You can find books and articles in a library by using the library's computer or cataloging system. If you are not sure how to use these resources, ask a librarian to help you. You can also use a computer to find many magazine articles and other articles written specifically for the Internet.

You are likely to find a lot more information than you can possibly use in your essay, so your first task is to narrow it down to what is likely to be most usable. Look at book and article titles. Look at book chapter titles, and examine the book's index to see if it contains information on the specific topic you want to write about. (For example, if you want to write about bullying and you find a book about school shootings, check the chapter titles and index to be sure it contains information about bullying before you bother to check out the book.)

For a five-paragraph essay, you do not need a great deal of supporting information, so quickly try to narrow down your materials to a few good books and magazine or Internet articles. You do not need dozens. You might even find that one or two good books or articles contain all the information you need.

You probably do not have time to read an entire book, so find the chapters or sections that relate to your topic, and skim these. When you find useful information, copy it onto a notecard or into a notebook. You should look for supporting facts, statistics, quotations, and examples.

Using the Internet

When you select your supporting information, it is important that you evaluate its source. This is especially important with information you find on the Internet. Because nearly anyone can put information on the Internet, there is as much bad information as good information online. Before using Internet information—or any information—try to determine whether the source seems to be reliable. Is the author or Internet site sponsored by a legitimate organization? Is it from a government source? Does the author have any special knowledge or training relating to the topic you are looking up? Does the article give any indication of where its information comes from?

Using Your Supporting Information

When you use supporting information from a book, article, interview, or other source, there are three important things to remember:

1. *Make it clear whether you are using a direct quotation or a paraphrase.* If you copy information directly from your source, you are quoting it. You must put quotation marks around the information and tell where the information comes from. If you put the information in your own words, you are paraphrasing it.

    Here is an example of a using a quotation:
    Author Lionel Shriver argues that the common motivation of all school shooters is a desire for fame. She states, "The public [school] shootings are often a cover for suicide, or for the private settling of scores with a parent or guardian. But a school shooting is reliably a bid for celebrity. As for murder-suicides like Jeff Weise's, even

posthumous notoriety must seem enthralling to someone who feels sufficiently miserable and neglected."[1]

Here is an example of a brief paraphrase of the same passage:

Author Lionel Shriver contends that although many school shootings are disguised attempts to commit suicide or exact revenge on parents, all of them are motivated by a desire for fame. School shooters who commit suicide are simply so miserable that they are attracted by the prospect of notoriety, even after death.

2. *Use the information fairly.* Be careful to use supporting information in the way the author intended it. For example, it is unfair to quote an author as saying, "Gun control works" when the author's complete quote is, "Gun control works to limit people's ability to defend themselves." This is called taking information out of context. Using that information as supporting evidence is unfair.

3. *Give credit where credit is due.* Giving credit is known as citing. You must use citations when you use someone else's information, but not every piece of supporting information needs a citation.

   - If the supporting information is general knowledge—that is, it can be found in many sources—you do not have to cite your source.
   - If you directly quote a source, you must cite it.
   - If you paraphrase information from a specific source, you must cite it.

If you do not use citations where you should, you are plagiarizing—or stealing—someone else's work.

Citing Your Sources

There are a number of ways to cite your sources. Your teacher will probably want you to do it in one of three ways:

   - Informal: As in the second example in number 1 above, you tell where you got the information in the same place you use it.

- Informal list: At the end of the article, place an unnumbered list of the sources you used. This tells the reader where, in general, you got your information.
- Formal: Use an endnote, as in the first example in number 1. (An endnote is generally placed at the end of an article or essay, although it may be located in different places depending on your teacher's requirements.)

Notes

1. Shriver, Lionel. "Dying to Be Famous." *New York Times* 27 Mar. 2005.

Using MLA Style to Create a Works Cited List

You will probably need to create a list of works cited for your paper. These include materials that you quoted from, relied heavily on, or consulted to write your paper. There are several different ways to structure these references. The following examples are based on Modern Language Association (MLA) style, one of the major citation styles used by writers.

Book Entries

For most book entries you will need the author's name, the book's title, where it was published, what company published it, and the year it was published. This information is usually found on the inside of the book. Variations on book entries include the following:

A book by a single author:
> Guest, Emma. *Children of AIDS: Africa's Orphan Crisis.* London: Sterling, 2003.

Two or more books by the same author:
> Friedman, Thomas L. *From Beirut to Jerusalem.* New York: Doubleday, 1989.
> ———. *The World Is Flat: A Brief History of the Twentieth Century.* New York: Farrar, Straus and Giroux, 2005.

A book by two or more authors:
> Pojman, Louis P., and Jeffrey Reiman. *The Death Penalty: For and Against.* Lanham, MD: Rowman & Littlefield, 1998.

A book with an editor:
> Friedman, Lauri S., ed. *At Issue: What Motivates Suicide Bombers?* San Diego, CA: Greenhaven, 2004.

Periodical and Newspaper Entries

Entries for sources found in periodicals and newspapers are cited a bit differently than books. For one, these sources usually have a title and a publication name. They also may have specific dates and page numbers. Unlike book entries, you do not need to list where newspapers or periodicals are published or what company publishes them.

An article from a periodical:
Snow, Keith Harmon. "State Terror in Ethiopia." *Z Magazine* June 2004: 33–35.

An unsigned article from a periodical:
"Broadcast Decency Rules." *Issues & Controversies On File* 30 Apr. 2004.

An article from a newspaper:
Constantino, Rebecca. "Fostering Love, Respecting Race." *Los Angeles Times* 14 Dec. 2002: B17.

Internet Sources

To document a source you found online, try to provide as much information on it as possible, including the author's name, the title of the document, the date of publication or of last revision, the URL, and your date of access.

A Web source:
Shyovitz, David. "The History and Development of Yiddish." Jewish Virtual Library 30 May 2005 < http://www.jewishvirtuallibrary.org/jsource/History/ yiddish.html >.

Your teacher will tell you exactly how information should be cited in your essay. Generally, the very least information needed is the original author's name and the name of the article or other publication.

Be sure you know exactly what information your teacher requires before you start looking for your supporting information so that you know what information to include with your notes.

Sample Essay Topics

Cause-and-Effect Essays

School Violence Is Caused by America's Gun Culture

School Violence Is Caused by Bullying in the Schools

Violence in the Media Causes School Violence

Violence in the Media Is Not to Blame for School Violence

Society's Expectations of Boys Causes School Shootings

The Effects of Bullying in the Schools

The Effects of School Shootings on Schools

The Effects of School Shootings on Communities

The Effects of School Shootings on Nonconformist Youths

The Chain of Events Leading to One School Shooting

The Chain of Events in a Community After a School Shooting

The Chain of Events in a Victim's Family After a School Shooting

The Chain of Events in a School After a School Shooting

The Chain of Events in the Life of a Student Wounded in a School Shooting

General Persuasive Essays

School Violence Is a Serious Problem

The Problem of School Violence Has Been Exaggerated

Anti-Bullying Programs Are Effective

Anti-Bullying Programs Are Unnecessary
Zero-Tolerance Policies Are Effective
Zero-Tolerance Policies Are Counterproductive
Gun Control Can Prevent School Violence
Gun Control Cannot Prevent School Violence
Parents Must Prevent Teens from Committing
  School Violence

Organizations to Contact

American Academy of Child and Adolescent Psychiatry (AACAP)
3615 Wisconsin Ave. NW, Washington, DC 20016-3007
(202) 966-7300 • Web site: www.aacap.org

AACAP is the leading national professional medical association committed to treating the 7 to 12 million American youths suffering from mental, behavioral, and developmental disorders.

Center for the Prevention of School Violence
1801 Mail Service Center, Raleigh, NC 27699-1801
(800) 299-6054 • (919) 733-3388, ext. 332
e-mail: jaclyn.myers@ncmail.net
Web site: www.ncdjjdp.org/cpsv

The Center for the Prevention of School Violence is a primary point of contact for information, programs, and research about school violence and its prevention. It provides information about all aspects of the problems that fall under the heading of school violence as well as information about strategies that are directed at solving these problems.

Fight Crime: Invest in Kids
2000 P St. NW, Suite 240, Washington, DC 20036
(202) 776-0027 • Web site: www.fightcrime.org

Fight Crime: Invest in Kids is a nonprofit organization led by more than twenty-five hundred police chiefs, sheriffs, prosecutors, victims of violence, and leaders of police officer associations. It conducts research and educates public-policy makers regarding the most effective ways to keep young people from becoming involved in crime.

Juvenile Law Center

The Philadelphia Bldg., 1315 Walnut St., 4th Fl.
Philadelphia, PA 19107 • (215) 625-0551
Web site: www.jlc.org

The center is a legal resource organization that advocates on behalf of children in the welfare, juvenile justice, and other public systems. It is dedicated to ending zero-tolerance policies in America's schools.

National Alliance for Safe Schools (NASS)

PO Box 290, Slanesville, WV 25445
(888) 510-6500 • (304) 496-8100
e-mail: nass@raven-villages.net
Web site: www.safeschools.org

Founded in 1977 by a group of school security directors, the National Alliance for Safe Schools was established to provide training, security assessments, and technical assistance to school districts interested in reducing school-based crime and violence.

National Association of School Resource Officers (NASRO)

14031 FM 315N, Chandler, TX 75758
(888) 31-NASRO • e-mail: resourcer@aol.com
Web site: www.nasro.org

The National Association of School Resource Officers is the first and only nonprofit training organization made up of liaison officers currently assigned to a school community. Its mission is to break down the barriers between law enforcement and youth.

National Institute of Justice (NIJ)
National Criminal Justice Reference Service (NCJRS)

PO Box 6000, Rockville, MD 20849-6000
(800) 851-3420 • e-mail: askncjrs@ncjrs.org
Web site: www.ncjrs.org

A component of the Office of Justice Programs of the U.S. Department of Justice, the NIJ supports research on crime, criminal behavior, and crime prevention. The NCJRS provides criminal justice information for researchers and other interested individuals.

National School Safety Center (NSSC)

141 Duesenberg Dr., Suite 11, Westlake Village, CA 91362
(805) 373-9977 • e-mail: info@nssc1.org
Web site: www.nssc1.org

The NSSC is a research organization that studies school crime and violence, including hate crimes. The center's mission is to focus national attention on cooperative solutions to problems that disrupt the educational process.

National Youth Violence Prevention Center

PO Box 10809, Rockville, MD 20849-0809
(866) SAFEYOUTH • Web site: www.safeyouth.org

The center was created by the U.S. Centers for Disease Control and Prevention to provide current information on youth violence. It maintains a toll-free hotline and distributes information on bullying and school violence, including fact sheets, statistics, and research bulletins.

Office of Juvenile Justice and Delinquency Prevention (OJJDP)

810 Seventh St. NW, Washington, DC 20531
(202) 307-5911 • e-mail: askjj@ojp.usdoj.gov
Web site: http://ojjdp.ncjrs.org

As the primary federal agency charged with monitoring and improving the juvenile justice system, the OJJDP develops and funds programs on juvenile justice. Among its goals are the prevention and control of illegal drug use and serious crime by juveniles.

U.S. Department of Education
Safe and Drug-Free Schools Program
400 Maryland Ave. SW, Washington, DC 20202
(800) USA-LEARN • (202) 260-3954
e-mail: customerservice@inet.ed.gov
Web site: www.ed.gov

The Safe and Drug-Free Schools Program is the U.S. Department of Education's primary vehicle for reducing drug, alcohol, and tobacco use as well as violence through education and prevention activities in America's schools.

Youth Crime Watch of America (YCWA)
9200 S. Dadeland Blvd., Suite 417, Miami, FL 33156
(305) 670-2409 • e-mail: ycwa@ycwa.org
Web site: www.ycwa.org

Youth Crime Watch of America is a nonprofit organization that assists youth in actively reducing crime and drug use in their schools and communities.

Bibliography

Books

Bochenek, Michael, *Hatred in the Hallways: Violence and Discrimination Against Lesbian, Gay, Bisexual, and Transgender Students in U.S. Schools*. New York: Human Rights Watch, 2001.

Casella, Ronnie, *At Zero Tolerance: Punishment, Prevention, and School Violence*. New York: Peter Lang, 2001.

Coloroso, Barbara, *The Bully, the Bullied, and the Bystander: From Preschool to High School—How Parents and Teachers Can Help Break the Cycle of Violence*. New York: HarperResource, 2003.

Davis, Stan, *Schools Where Everyone Belongs: Practical Strategies for Reducing Bullying*. Wayne, ME: Stop Bullying Now, 2003.

Fein, R., et al., *Threat Assessment in Schools: A Guide to Managing Threatening Situations and to Creating Safe School Climates*. Washington, DC: U.S. Department of Education, Office of Elementary and Secondary Education, Safe and Drug-Free Schools Program and U.S. Secret Service, National Threat Assessment Center, 2002.

Fight Crime: Invest in Kids, *Bullying Prevention Is Crime Prevention*. Washington, DC: Fight Crime: Invest in Kids, 2003.

Kaplan, H. Roy, *Failing Grades: How Schools Breed Frustration, Anger, and Violence, and How to Prevent It*. Lanham, MD: Scarecrow Education, 2004.

National Research Council and Institute of Medicine, *Deadly Lessons: Understanding Lethal School Violence*. Ed. Mark H. Moore et al. Washington, DC: National Academies Press, 2003.

Newman, Katherine S., *Rampage: The Social Roots of School Shootings*. New York: Basic Books, 2004.

Orr, Tamra, *Violence in Our Schools: Halls of Hope, Halls of Fear*. New York: Franklin Watts, 2003.

Peretti, Frank, *No More Victims!* Nashville, TN: Thomas Nelson, 2001.

Sampson, Rana, *Bullying in Schools.* Washington, DC: U.S. Department of Justice, 2004.

Sheras, Peter L., *Your Child: Bully or Victim? Understanding and Ending Schoolyard Tyranny.* New York: Fireside, 2002.

Periodicals

Beger, Randall R., "Expansion of Police Power in Public Schools and the Vanishing Rights of Students," *Social Justice,* Spring/Summer 2002.

Best, Joel, "Monster Hype: How a Few Isolated Tragedies—and Their Supposed Causes—Were Turned into a National 'Epidemic,'" *Education Next,* Summer 2002.

Blank, Jonah, "The Kid No One Noticed: Guns, He Concluded, Would Get His Classmates' Attention," *U.S. News & World Report,* October 12, 1998.

Chaltain, Sam, and Molly McCloskey, "Red Lake Shooting: No More Quick Fixes," *USA Today,* March 30, 2005.

Chapman, Steve, "The Odd Silence After the School Shootings," *Chicago Tribune,* March 24, 2005.

Connoly, Ceci, and Dana Hedgpeth, "Shooter Described as Deeply Disturbed," *Washington Post,* March 24, 2005.

Donahue, Marilyn Cram, "Back Off Bullies!" *Current Health2,* April/May, 2004.

Ehrenkranz, Penny Lockwood, "To Snitch or Not to Snitch," *Listen,* April 1, 2004.

Fox, James Alan, "How to Avoid Columbine II," *USA Today,* April 19, 2004.

Fuentes, Annette, "Discipline and Punish: Zero Tolerance Policies Have Created a 'Lockdown Environment' in Schools," *Nation,* December 15, 2003.

Greenya, John, "Bullying: Are Schools Doing Enough to Solve the Problem?" *CQ Researcher*, February 4, 2005.

Juvonen, Jaana, "Myths and Facts About Bullying in Schools," *Behavioral Health Management*, March 1, 2005.

Labash, Matt, "Beating Up on Bullies," *Weekly Standard*, February 24, 2003.

Lady Liberty, "Who's Crazy Now?" *OpinionEditorials.com*, April 4, 2005.

Newman, Katherine S., "Too Close for Comfort," *New York Times*, April 17, 2004.

Paulson, Amanda, "Why School Violence Is Declining," *Christian Science Monitor*, December 6, 2004.

Sweeney, Emily, "Mistaken Identity: These Are Dark Days for Goths, Who Say It's Wrong to Tie Them to School Violence," *Boston Globe*, October 14, 2004.

Thompson, Jack, "More Columbines? Video Games and School Shootings," *Washington Times*, July 2, 2004.

Web Sites

End Zero Tolerance (http://endzerotolerance.com). This site is a forum for those who oppose the use of zero-tolerance policies in public schools. It offers information on zero tolerance and links to research, commentary, and news articles on the topic.

Stop Bullying Now! (http://stopbullyingnow.hrsa.gov). A government Web site designed to help children and their parents deal with bullying in the schools. It offers fact sheets on bullying and advice for children faced with bullying behavior.

Time Line of Recent Worldwide School Shootings (www.infoplease.com/ipa/A0777958.html). This page, maintained by Information Please, is an annotated list of school shootings around the world from 1996 to the present arranged in chronological order.

Youth Violence Prevention Resource Center (www.safe
youth.org). The Web site of a program sponsored by the
U.S. Centers for Disease Control and Prevention, this site
offers information and links to additional resources on
school violence. It contains fact sheets on school violence and bullying geared specifically to teens.

Index

Picture Credits

Cover: AP/Wide World Photos
AP/Wide World Photos, 38, 41, 43, 47
© Emely/ZEFA/CORBIS, 31
© Najlah Feanny/CORBIS, 14, 48
Getty Images, 19, 22, 25
© Scott Houston/CORBIS, 35
© James Leynse/CORBIS, 28
© Reuters/CORBIS, 27
© Sygma/CORBIS, 12
Victor Habbick Visions, 13, 42

About the Editor

Scott Barbour received a bachelor's degree in English and a master's degree in social work from San Diego State University. He has worked as a case manager and counselor with the severely mentally ill. He is currently a senior acquisitions editor for Greenhaven Press, for whom he has edited numerous books on social issues, historical topics, and current events.